Beauty and the Beast

A pantomime

Book and lyrics by
David Cregan

Music by Brian Protheroe

GW01326081

Samuel French – London
New York – Sydney – Toronto – Hollywood

© 1988 BY DAVID CREGAN (BOOK AND LYRICS)

1. *This play is fully protected under the Copyright Laws of the British Commonwealth of Nations, the United States of America and all countries of the Berne and Universal Copyright Conventions.*

2. *All rights, including Stage, Motion Picture, Radio, Television, Public Reading and Translation into Foreign Languages, are strictly reserved.*

3. **No part of this publication may lawfully be reproduced in ANY form or by any means—photocopying, typescript, recording (including video-recording), manuscript, electronic, mechanical, or otherwise—or be transmitted or stored in a retrieval system, without prior permission.**

4. Rights of Performance by Amateurs are controlled by SAMUEL FRENCH LTD, 52 FITZROY STREET, LONDON W1P 6JR, and they, or their authorized agents, issue licences to amateurs to give performances of this play on payment of a fee. **This fee is subject to contract and subject to variation at the sole discretion of Samuel French Ltd.**

5. Licences are issued subject to the understanding that it shall be made clear in all advertising matter that the audience will witness an amateur performance; that the names of the authors of the plays shall be included on all announcements and on all programmes; and that the integrity of the author's work will be preserved.

The publication of this play does not imply that it is necessarily available for performance by amateurs or professionals, either in the British Isles or Overseas. Amateurs and professionals considering a production are strongly advised in their own interests to apply to the appropriate agents for consent before starting rehearsals or booking a theatre or hall.

ISBN 0 573 06481 4

BEAUTY AND THE BEAST

First presented at the Theatre Royal, Stratford East, on 1st December 1987, with the following cast of characters:

Dolores, a wicked fairy	Angela Bruce
King Tom, later **The Beast**	Christopher Snell
Candy, a good fairy	Lavinia Bertram
Snowdrop, her apprentice	Debbie Roza
Mr James Smith, a rich, old man	John Halstead
Ivy, his daughter	Jackie Downey
Jacintha, his other daughter	Judy Damas
Beauty, his youngest daughter	Madeline Adams
Mrs Buller, the housekeeper	Christopher Owen
Arnold, the footman	Paul Barber
Sir Simon Prettyface, a suitor	Alex Richardson
Sir Thomas Funnywit, another suitor	Kraig Thornber

Director Philip Hedley
Assistant Director Dev Sagoo
Musical Director Dave Brown
Choreographer Joanne Campbell
Set and Costume Designer Geoff Rose
Assistant Designer Philippe Brandt
Lighting Designer Stephen Watson
Sound Designer Derrick Zieba
Production Manager Bob Irwin
Chief Electrician Chris Davey
Sound Operator Niki Lawrence
Stage Manager Sara Grimshaw
Deputy Stage Manager Beccy Fawcett
Assistant Stage Manager (Book) Nigel Rhodes
Stage Carpenter Joe Gallagher
Wardrobe Supervisor Joanne Pearce
Associate Designer Jenny Tiramani

SYNOPSIS OF SCENES

ACT I

ACT II

MUSICAL NUMBERS

ACT I

1.	Coronation Song	All
2.	A Rose is a Rose	Beauty
3.	We're Rich (Happy)	Ivy, Jacintha, Beauty
4.	I'd Give Every Breath in my Body for You	Beauty, Arnold, Mrs Buller, Mr Smith
5.	The Haymaking Cake Walk	Beauty, Mr Smith, Mrs Buller, Ivy, Jacintha, Arnold
6.	The Bicycle Spell	Candy
7.	He's Gone Down the Drain in a Rage	Dolores, Snowdrop, Candy
8.	Though Dead I Kept my Word	Mrs Buller, Ivy, Jacintha, Mr Smith, Arnold
9.	I'll Somehow Shine	Beast

ACT II

10.	Now We're Hitched	Ivy, Jacintha, Sir Thomas, Sir Simon, Mrs Buller, Mr Smith, Arnold
11.	Pull Your Socks Up	Mrs Buller, Arnold, Mr Smith
12.	In a Week	Beauty, Beast
12A.	In a Week (Reprise)	Beast
13.	Sleep Sweetly and Dream	Dolores, Candy, Snowdrop
14.	Playing Silly Games	Sir Simon, Sir Thomas, Beauty
15.	Beast Noises	Snowdrop, Candy, Mrs Buller
16.	Just the Way You Are	Company

The vocal score is available separately from Samuel French Ltd

Pd: Milkyway User 090

Pd: Spooks User 093

St.: Harp Multi 047

funfare -BrassTek User 081

Spell → St: Fillatte User 089

Rich (happy) — Multi ~ III Et: fiddle?

Kiss scene → Pd: VS—Val User 095 straight

Brass Tek 081

Scene 1 ~~for~~ fanfare

Scene 2 for Dolores

ACT I

SCENE 1

A Coronation in Belldrovia

A great flash and crack of thunder. Dolores is revealed, glamorous but bald. (Probably drinking gin, but that's optional)

Dolores I am Dolores, a wicked and wonderfully selfish fairy, and I am about to choose my two hundred and seventy-third husband. All the others have died, mostly in rather funny ways, and the one I want now is back there. He's a nice fresh young king, just being crowned, and you might like to have a look at him to see if he isn't the prettiest fellow a girl like me could want.

Trumpets. The Coronation of the young and good-looking King Tom is revealed. Tom wears glasses and as well as being crowned is busy signing things so that there is some difficulty getting his crown on. He hands things to his Courtiers. A choir is behind him

There. King Tom of Belldrovia

Courtiers ⎫
Choir ⎭ (*together*) King Tom of Belldrovia.

Dolores (*as she leaves*) Yummy!

Dolores exits

Song 1: Coronation Song

All   Vivat Tom!
     Pom, pom, pom!
     Highly intelligent and goes like a bomb
     Always at work like a busy little bee.
     Long live his royal productivity!

Tom Thank you, everyone, lovely. Will someone please get the royal study ready so I can go and invent important things?
Courtier Yes, Your Majesty.
Tom And will someone else arrange a lot of visits to my subjects because I haven't met them yet and I want to know what they're like.
Another Courtier Yes, Your Majesty.

There is another flash and Dolores is revealed beside Tom

Tom Good heavens. Are *you* one of my subjects?
Dolores Marry me.

Tom I don't do that sort of thing, I'm afraid.
Dolores Marry me.
Tom I'm just too busy at the moment.
Dolores Marry me!
Tom (*irritated*) Someone take this lady away.
Dolores AAAAAAAH! You're not normal!

There is a great crash and the King and all the Courtiers are frozen. Strange sounds

No-one, but no-one refuses to do what I ask and gets away with it. As punishment you will be turned into a creature of such appalling ugliness that no-one will want to come near it let alone play with it. And this torment will go on for ever and ever in a lonely and empty castle in the Doom Laden Woods with no-one in it to talk to where your friends very shortly will carry you ... Unless (I like to give people hope, it makes it worse) you persuade a very good and very beautiful young girl to come along and marry you.
Courtier Which of course, being ugly, he won't.
Another Courtier Waste of a really nice king.
Dolores Drag him away while I spell out his fate.
Courtiers Where?
Dolores There!

The outline of a grim and gloomy castle glimmers into view. Much shuddering

Tom Am I to be all alone there?
Dolores Yes. If you won't have my love, then have my hate!

Against their will a couple of Courtiers drag the King away as she chants the curse. His face and body assume horrible distortions as he disappears into the mist suggesting even more appalling things are about to happen to him, as indeed they will

Dolores' Curse

(*Chanting*)   Farewell, sweet face, farewell fond smile,
Transformed to features especially vile;
Your hands to hooves, your feet to claws,
Your voice to harsh and raging roars;
Your skin to feathers mixed up with scales,
As scratchy as sandpaper, hard as nails;
Be bitter, and angry, lonely and sad ...

He has disappeared. One lonely plaintive roar

Oh, I feel better when I've been bad,

(*Speaking*) And that's him settled for eternity.

She laughs and is gone

Candy, a very blonde, healthy, slightly too-old-for-it good fairy, and her apprentice, Snowdrop, who is eager, enter

Candy Do not worry Kingdom of Belldrovia. Help is at hand.

Snowdrop It certainly is.

Candy I am Candy, the most well-balanced of all good fairies, and I was passing by with Snowdrop, my apprentice——

Snowdrop Me.

Candy —and we saw that and we thought it was absolutely foul, didn't we?

Snowdrop Yes.

Candy (*to the audience*) And didn't you?

Audience response

Didn't you?

More response

Snowdrop You did.

Candy Yes, right, exactly. Dolores is the absolute pits, isn't she. Isn't she?

Responses as before

Snowdrop She is.

Candy Yes, right exactly. But don't worry. We'll find a thoroughly decent young girl to go and marry that poor king and everything will turn out beautifully. Snowdrop will do it as part of her training, won't you, dear.

Snowdrop Candy, my first real job!

Candy So enthusiastic. Now, do we know anybody suitable for a young king turned into a beast?

Snowdrop Yes. One of the Smith girls!

Candy Oh, the Smith girls. Such a nice family, and the youngest one is awfully kind and good.

Snowdrop They call her Beauty.

Candy Let's have a look, shall we?

The Smith drawing-room is revealed with Mr Smith and Beauty at the harpsichord

Snowdrop There she is. Beauty.

Candy Yes, right, exactly.

They exit as the next scene begins

SCENE 2

Mr James Smith's drawing-room, notable for being light and airy. It has a harpsichord in it and Beauty is playing on it. Mr Smith is listening to her enraptured. He is an elderly looking man with long straggly hair. Arnold the footman is dusting things and also listening and perhaps humming

Song 2: A Rose is a Rose

Beauty   A rose is a rose
                      And by any other name

It would probably smell as sweet.
It would almost certainly
Look the same,
Extremely pretty and neat.
But there's one rose I know that I
Alone am expected to see!
It's the gift of a love, a miracle rose,
And a rose that was grown for me.

She finishes

Mr Smith Oh lovely!
Arnold Oh miss!
Mr Smith Play it again, Beauty.

She does as they hum with her round the harpsichord

Candy and Snowdrop appear unseen in the room

Candy Charming, dear, and how are you going to get her out to the Doom Laden Woods?
Snowdrop Give me time. There's a housekeeper who might help.
Candy A housekeeper?
Snowdrop You have to use what's available, Candy. It's the first rule for interfering with humans.
Candy I do know.
Mrs Buller (*off*) What's that?
Snowdrop Quick. Here she comes.

They hide themselves away somewhere

Candy (*as they do*) Not overdressed, is she.

Mrs Buller, the housekeeper, enters. She is tall and thin, with her hair done in a bun. She wears a long black dress and has a belt with keys on it. She has a watch on her breast, like nurses do

Mrs Buller And what's going on here? It's not harpsichord time for another two minutes. Open those curtains to let in the light.
Arnold (*doing it*) Curtains to let in the light.
Mrs Buller Table for the chocolates and the eyeshades. *fluttering fans.*
Beauty Chocolates and eyeshades. *fluttering fans.*
Mrs Buller (*to Beauty*) You sit still. You're not supposed to be here yet. (*To the audience*) Oh, I have my work cut out keeping things in order, here. Take my eyes off them for a second and there's chaos. Chaos!
Mr Smith Mrs Buller.
Mrs Buller Quiet!
Mr Smith It's my house.
Mrs Buller And you take charge of it when I tell you.
Beauty Never mind, Father.
Mr Smith She depresses me.
Mrs Buller (*to the audience*) Now, I'm Mrs Buller, the housekeeper. Hello. I said, I'm Mrs Buller, the housekeeper. Hello. That's better.

Mr Smith She's not the housekeeper, she's the dictator.

Beauty But she keeps things tidy.

Mrs Buller (*to someone in the audience*) Don't scratch your ear, darling, or it'll fall off and we'll have a mess. Now, I look after the Smith family, and I keep order because Mr Smith can't. I'm trying to teach him how but at the moment he's hopeless, aren't you, hopeless.

Mr Smith Yes, hopeless.

Arnold Hopeless.

Mrs Buller Hopeless.

Beauty But lovely.

Mrs Buller If it weren't for me, there'd be dirty washing piled up to the ceiling, and every sink would be inches deep in filth, and don't scratch your neighbour's ear or that'll fall off, too, and we'll be up to our elbows in ears.

Beauty Mrs Buller!

Mrs Buller Now, I'm quite a nice person—several people have liked me in my time—about three, I think—and this is Arnold, who does the heavy work, don't you——

Arnold And the light work.

Mrs Buller Yes, and this——

Arnold And the medium work.

Mrs Buller This——

Arnold In fact all the work, if you want the truth.

Mrs Buller Arnold! A place for everyone, and everyone in their place, and that's yours over there, standing still as a lamp-post in silence and the truth has nothing to do with you. Now this, this is Beauty—look at her— Beauty by name and Beauty by nature.

Beauty That's right.

Mrs Buller She's Mr Smith's youngest and most wonderful daughter whom I very nearly love.

Beauty Everybody does, especially Papa.

Mr Smith Yes.

Mrs Buller You can kiss me later when I have a second, but now it's order giving. Over here, Arnold—Arnold!—and——

Arnold } (*together*) One two three—good-morning, master, what
Mrs Buller } d'you want us to do?

Mr Smith She always does this, and I don't know what to say.

Mrs Buller Tell us what we must do!

Arnold We know what we must do.

Mrs Buller But he has to learn to say it.

Beauty Poor Papa. Do what Mrs Buller says.

Mrs Buller Say, "Go and get my other daughters."

Mr Smith Would you mind very much if you went to——

Mrs Buller Not would you mind very much—"Go and get the others!"

Arnold Right.

He goes

Mrs Buller Not yet! *He* has to say it!

Mr Smith Go and get——
Mrs Buller Too late. As always, everything wrong, muddle, mess, chaos, and now it's harpsichord time so start playing.

Beauty does

And you lean on it and look elegant in case we have visitors.

Mr Smith is engrossed with Beauty

Go on. Like they do in pictures, charming and proud. (*She does it herself*) Like this. Go on. Do it!
Mr Smith Quiet!
Mrs Buller Oh! Not bad!
Mr Smith I'm awfully sorry, Mrs Buller. I didn't mean——
Mrs Buller No, no, have another go if you like. Come on.

They proceed to encourage and apologize while Candy and Snowdrop appear again

Candy I don't see what help she can be to anybody.
Snowdrop (*thoughtful*) She's bossy.
Candy Yes, right, exactly.
Snowdrop Perhaps that's it. I'm beginning to get a plan and it's amazingly subtle.
Arnold (*off*) Miss Ivy and Miss Jacintha Smith.
Snowdrop The other sisters. They might be useful.
Candy (*as they hide again*) You can overdo subtlety, Snowdrop.

Arnold pushes on Ivy and Jacintha, two very pampered ladies who eat chocs and put on eyeshades as required. They are in two chaises-longues

Ivy Stop that racket!
Jacintha Harpsichords, harpsichords, it's nothing but harpsichords in this house.

Beauty stops playing, Mrs Buller looks confused and glances at her watch

Ivy Arrange us properly, Arnold, so we look our best.
Jacintha And take away the sunlight before my skin fades.

Mrs Buller rushes to the curtains

Beauty You haven't seen your skin for years, Jacintha.
Jacintha Who said that?
Beauty Me.
Ivy Uncross my legs, will you?
Jacintha Was that our goody-goody sister being spiteful?
Beauty Not spiteful, truthful.
Mrs Buller (*to Mr Smith*) Beauty is never spiteful. Tell them.
Mr Smith If you played the harpsichord as well as——
Ivy If we want music, Father, we pay people to play it for us.
Jacintha And if we want to hear stories, we pay people to read them to us.
Ivy And if we want to eat things we pay people to feed us.

Jacintha Because, we're rich.

Ivy And beautiful.

Jacintha And it's our business to sit around all day——

Jacintha ⎫
Ivy ⎭ (*together*) Thus!

They lie in their version of beauty

Jacintha Because we're the Smith girls.

Ivy We don't do anything for ourselves.

Song 3: We're Rich (Happy)

Ivy ⎫
Jacintha ⎭
We're terribly, terribly beautiful
And terribly, terribly rich;
We don't have to do the washing up
Don't have to sew a stitch;
We don't have to do the ironing,
Or even clean the loo;
Our life is full of the awful things
We never have to do.

CHORUS (Note: the word "happy" in this chorus is sung by Beauty and follows the word "rich". It is not sung at the same time as the word "rich"

	'Cos we're rich.
Beauty	Happy
Ivy ⎫ **Jacintha** ⎭	Rich
Beauty	Happy
Ivy ⎫ **Jacintha** ⎭	Beautiful and rich
	Never move a muscle
	Even though we have an itch
	No-one can imagine
	Just how blissfully we drift.
	Our hands are full of fingers
	That we never have to lift.
	'Cos we're rich
Beauty	Happy
Ivy ⎫ **Jacintha** ⎭	Rich
Beauty	Happy
Ivy ⎫ **Jacintha** ⎭	Beautiful and rich.
Beauty	We're terribly, terribly lucky
	With a Pa who's terribly kind.
Mr Smith	With terribly lovely daughters.
Ivy ⎫ **Jacintha** ⎭	Though there's one who's a terrible bind.

Beauty   We paint and play and dance all day
And sing till the moon is blue.
Our life is full of the lovely things
We're lucky we can do.

*CHORUS (This is sung by everyone present, though once again the single
word, this time "lucky", is sung by Beauty alone)*

All	'Cos we're rich
Beauty	Lucky
All	Rich
Beauty	Lucky
All	Beautiful and rich.
Beauty	Life is a tumble of happiness.
Ivy **Jacintha** }	And she's the only hitch.
Beauty	No-one will believe that there's so
Many things that I'm wanting to have a go at.
But I never have the time—
All	'Cos we're rich
Beauty	Lucky
All	Rich
Beauty	Lucky
All	Beautiful and rich.
Arnold **Mrs Buller** }	They're terribly, terribly lazy.
Ivy **Jacintha** }	We'll marry extremely well.
Arnold **Mrs Buller** }	They can't even blow their noses.
Ivy **Jacintha** }	To chaps who are terribly swell.
Arnold **Mrs Buller** }	They'll drive their husbands potty.
Ivy **Jacintha** }	They'll be lords from high above.
We'll marry to live in their palaces
But certainly not for love.

*CHORUS (Note: the single word "lazy" is sung by everyone except the two
sisters and eventually even Mrs Buller)*

Ivy **Jacintha** }	Not for love
Others	Lazy
Ivy **Jacintha** }	Love
Others	Lazy

Ivy	We've no time for love.
Jacintha	Having to think of someone else In case you get the shove.
Beauty	I'll only take a man that I Can love with all my might.
Ivy	She won't be rich and comfy
Jacintha	And we think it serves her right
	Love
Beauty	Lazy
Ivy	Love
Jacintha	
Beauty	Lazy
Ivy	We've no time for love.
Jacintha	
All	'Cos we're rich
Beauty	Happy
All	Rich
Beauty	Happy
All	Beautiful and rich.

A bell rings very loudly as if at the front door

Ivy Oh, lovely. That'll be the first man of the day, come to propose. Go and get him, Arnold, so we can turn him down and watch him squirm.

Arnold goes out

The two good fairies appear again, led by the enthusiastic Snowdrop

Snowdrop Got it. Rich marriages. We need a disguise.
Candy At my age?
Snowdrop I'm moving fast, now.

They have gone

Beauty I think you should be nice to this person whoever he is.
Mrs Buller Yes, you should.
Jacintha Why?
Beauty Well some of them are very fond of you.
Ivy That's bad luck on them, then isn't it.
Mrs Buller No, it isn't. It's very selfish, and it's very untidy and it's got to stop.
Ivy *(together)* Eh?
Jacintha
Mrs Buller Aren't you going to make them accept these nice young men who come to propose?
Mr Smith Oh, I couldn't do that.
Mrs Buller Well, I could, so today's the day they choose their husbands and get things properly in order.

Ivy What are you talking about?

Jacintha Give her the sack, Father.

Sir Simon Prettyface and Sir Thomas Funnywit arrive, foppish young men whose names explain their pretensions to existence. Arnold shows them in

Mrs Buller Now, who are you?

Sir Simon Sir Simon Prettyface, the gorgeous one.

Sir Thomas Sir Thomas Funnywit, the clever one, hahaha.

Mrs Buller Come to propose?

Sir Simon }
Sir Thomas } *(together)* Yes.

Mrs Buller On your knees.

Sir Simon }
Sir Thomas } *(together)* What?

Mrs Buller Knees. Knees, knees, knees.

Arnold Knees, come on.

Mrs Buller Which ones d'you want?

Sir Simon }
Sir Thomas } *(together)* We both want that one. *(They point at Beauty)*

Arnold No good, I'm afraid.

Mrs Buller No, she's too lovely for anyone round here.

Beauty I'm afraid I am, aren't I, Papa?

Mr Smith Yes, she is.

Arnold Yes.

Mrs Buller So it's Ivy or Jacintha or home to Mother.

Arnold Speak up. Who's for which?

Jacintha Father, we can't. They're terribly suburban.

Sir Simon We've decided.

Sir Thomas I'm for this, and he's for that.

Sir Simon }   Will you make us the happiest of men by letting
Sir Thomas } *(together)*   us marry you for your money?

Ivy }
Jacintha } *(together)* No.

Mrs Buller Yes.

Ivy }
Jacintha } *(together)* What?

Mrs Buller Yes, you will make them the happiest of men or you'll have no supper tonight, and you'll have to cut my toe-nails before going to bed.

Arnold And you'll have to learn to read.

Ivy But it's the wrong way round.

Jacintha We're supposed to marry them for their money.

Ivy Speak to her, Father.

Mrs Buller Don't you dare.

Mr Smith No.

Mrs Buller And you two get up and say thank you.

Sir Simon }
Sir Thomas } *(rising, together)* Thank you.

Mrs Buller Just announce their forthcoming marriages, Arnold, and let's get it all tidy and out of the way. (*To the audience*) And I've told you about ears.

Arnold I announce the forthcoming marriage of Mr Smith's elder and very selfish daughters to two fairly repugnant young men and I hope they go and live somewhere else.

Mrs Buller Excellent. And if anyone knows any reason why these four people should not get married, speak up or here for ever after hold your peace and we can get the whole thing settled and do the hoovering.

Snowdrop marches in dressed as a lawyer, followed by Candy, similarly dressed

Snowdrop I know a reason.

Mrs Buller What?

Arnold Who let you in?

Snowdrop Are you Mr James Smith, the fabulously rich merchant?

Mr Smith I think so.

Snowdrop I have to tell you there has been a most dreadful disaster in the merchant world and you have lost your entire fortune. (*She hands over documents to Mr Smith*)

Beauty Papa!

Jacintha You're joking.

Snowdrop I'm a lawyer. I don't joke.

Sir Thomas } (*together*) { Oh.
Sir Simon } { Goodness.

Ivy Let's see.

Jacintha And me.

Beauty There, there, Papa.

Candy Is this true?

Snowdrop Absolutely. I've ruined him.

Candy I thought you were being subtle.

Sir Simon (*to Snowdrop*) Ought we to go, d'you think?

Snowdrop Pretty quick, if I were you. He's so broke he won't have enough to keep you in beauty spots.

Sir Simon Are there people that poor?

Sir Thomas Yes, I've seen them and they're horrid.

Sir Simon Well, I'm only taking mine for better, not for worse, so I'm off.

Sir Thomas Lucky escape, really. Thanks for being timely.

He tips Snowdrop and they leave

Mrs Buller (*seeing them*) You half-hearted, lily-livered nincompoops! You wet lettuces. You dead hens. (*To Snowdrop*) And you haven't wiped your boots properly. What does it say?

Jacintha Which are the letters and which are the numbers?

Mr Smith It says all my money's gone, that's what it says.

Beauty Oh, Papa.

Ivy But it can't have. You've always had money, you've given us everything we've asked for, made us into the beautiful creatures we are ...

Beauty He's lovely.

Jacintha You've messed everything up, haven't you, spent everything on presents and pretty clothes and jewels.
Beauty No!
Ivy Listening to the harpsichord when you should've been working ...
Jacintha You've let us down.
Ivy Yes, lifted us up, and then let us down.
Arnold Don't talk to your father like that.
Mrs Buller No.
Beauty It's horrid.
Mr Smith But it's true.
Ivy
Jacintha } (*together*) It is.
Mr Smith And I'm so sorry.
Jacintha Sorry? Who's going to marry a girl with a father who's sorry?
Ivy Simon? Scrumptious Simon. (*As she begins to run off*) I love you Simon, don't go.

She runs off

Jacintha Thomas! Wait for me. It's Juicy Jacintha! Wait!

She runs off

Mrs Buller Trollops!
Arnold Push your own chairs in future.
Mr Smith They'll have to. We're poor.
Snowdrop Frightfully poor. BUT—you still have your little place in the country near the Doom Laden Woods, so you can go and live there.
Candy Oh, their little place in the country near the Doom Laden Woods—that's very clever of you, Snowdrop.
Snowdrop Thank you.
Beauty It'll be lovely, Papa.
Candy Sorry to bring you misery at such a happy time, but I expect everything will turn out for the best in the end.
Mrs Buller Do you indeed.
Candy (*leaving with Snowdrop*) It usually does. We'll see ourselves out.

They leave

Arnold Pity you ever saw yourselves in.
Beauty (*comforting her father*) Don't cry. We love the country, and we'll all be together, so we'll manage beautifully.
Mr Smith But I'm a fool, I tell you, a fool.
Beauty Yes, but you're a lovely fool, and I do love you. Papa? I love you so enormously, you just can't imagine.

Arnold weeps a bit at this sweet sight

Mrs Buller Don't go getting tears all over the carpet, Arnold. Get out the dust sheets.

Song 4: I'd Give Every Breath in my Body for You

Beauty   It can't be denied
That your mind isn't wide
And you're everyone's fool
They can take for a ride.

The rich in the ranks
Of the boys in the banks
Say you're short in your marbles
And thick as two planks.

But oh I adore you, inane as you are,
Ridiculous, crumpled and stupid Papa.
So lift your grey head, though it's empty all through.
I'll give every breath in my body for you.

Arnold   ⎫   His thinking is slight
Mrs Buller ⎭   And he doesn't know quite
If he's coming or going,
Nor tell day from night.

His heart may be sound,
His affection renowned,
But in business he's just
Nineteen bob in the pound.

But oh she adores him, the fool that he is,
Though lacking in oomph and deficient in fizz.
So lift your grey head, though it's empty all through
She'd give every breath in her body for you.

Mr Smith   Though doing my best
I have lost, they attest,
Not only my shirt but my
Pants and my vest.

No longer I clutch
Golden sovereigns and such—
You're all I have left and
I love you so much.

Beauty   But oh, I adore you, inane as you are,
Ridiculous, crumpled and stupid Papa.
So lift your grey head, though it's empty all through,
I'd give every breath in my body—

All   And oh she adores you, you foolish old thing;
A withered old puppet without any string.

All (*but*   So hold up your head, though it's empty all through.
Mr Smith)

Mr Smith ⎫
Beauty   ⎭   I'd give every breath, every breath in my body for you.

Beauty hugs her father

SCENE 3

The Horrid Hammock

A frontcloth. On one side of the stage is Dolores in her Horrid Hammock. This is made up of dead animals and girls' pig-tails and is held by two vaguely human-looking tree trunks. She is lying in this hammock and is drinking from a glass which is connected to a great vat of gin

Snowdrop comes to the other side to speak to the audience

Snowdrop It's all going quite nicely, now you see——
Dolores You don't fool me, Bluebell.
Snowdrop Snowdrop.
Dolores You're moving those dismal Smith girls nearer to the forest where my beast lives, aren't you?
Snowdrop We've been told never to speak to you, Dolores.
Dolores And you're hoping that priggish little Beauty will blunder into his lonely castle and marry him, aren't you. Aren't you, Sunbeam?
Snowdrop Snowdrop.
Dolores Well, she may blunder into his castle but she won't marry him. Even his mother wouldn't love him the way I've made him look and his temper is awful. Listen!

A howl. Dolores laughs

Snowdrop (*shocked*) You're pleased.
Dolores Yes.

Candy appears

Candy Goodness will conquer all, Dolores. Come along, dear.
Dolores Oh, it's Arkela.
Candy Who?
Dolores There's more to life than goodness. Want a sweet, gel?
Snowdrop Oh, thank you very much.
Candy Snowdrop! You don't know where it's been.
Snowdrop Oh, no sorry.
Candy It's probably filled with Yuk Potion that will turn you into a beast.
Dolores (*grinning at the audience*) Want to find out if they do turn you into beasts? (*She begins to throw them into the audience*) Go on, just try them.
Candy No, don't. They'll turn you into beasts.
Dolores Oh no they won't.
Candy
Snowdrop } (*together*) Oh yes they will.

Et cetera

Dolores There's only one way to find out. You just suck them and see.
Snowdrop Oh, Candy, they've started.
Candy Keep your head, dear. I've an anti-beast spell that never fails if you

use it in time. (*She makes gestures*) Sweet, sweet, what a treat, do not harm them as they eat. There you are dear, they'll be all right now.

Snowdrop Is that it?

Candy Strong and simple, like me.

Dolores You really boring other worldly thing, you. It would've been wonderful to have the whole place filled with horrors. I'd better try again later, hadn't I, with some better, stronger Yuk Potion.

Snowdrop You won't be able to do anything if I get this story going my way. We'd better hurry and see how my plan is working in the little place in the country near the Doom Laden Woods.

Dolores You can't set an apprentice against my experience and hope to win.

Candy Well, let's see, shall we?

They exit as the frontcloth rises on . . .

SCENE 4

The little place in the country

There are present Mr Smith, Mrs Buller, Arnold, Ivy, Jacintha and Beauty. There is a sense of bedragglement about the two older sisters, but the others are benefiting from the healthy life of the countryside, to such an extent that they are singing: The Haymaking Cake Walk

Song 5: The Haymaking Cake Walk

All   Haymaking,
Heaving all the grass in the air.
We're making hay-ho.
~~Stook staking~~ Straw shaking
Catching all the ~~straws~~ seeds in our hair,
We're ridin' high.
Sheep dipping,
Sorting all the fluff into flocks,
We're nuts in May-oh.
Fleece clipping,
Growing all the wool for our socks,
My friends and I.
Milk squeezing, buttering and cheesing,
Down the meadow, birds and beesing.
We're licking nature into wonderful shape
Just making hay.

Dance break

Ivy   }
Jacintha }   Muck shifting
Clearing every pile in the place,
We don't half pong-oh.
Bale lifting,

Till we're sweating red in the face,
All steaming hot.
Scare crowing,
Like to take each bird by the neck
And stretch it long-oh.
Seed sowing,
We'd take every bushel and peck
And flush the lot.
Long sunny days with bees and honey—
You can have 'em, we want money.
We long for bustles and the rustle of silk
Not making hay.

All   Haymaking
Heaving all the grass in the air
We're making hay-ho.
Stook staking,
Catching all the straws in our hair,
We're riding high.
Milk squeezing, buttering and cheesing,
Down the meadow birds and beesin'.
We're licking nature into wonderful shape
Just making hay.
We're makin' hay.

Mrs Buller Right, enough nonsense. Into line you moping minnies.

Arnold Into line for the day's orders.

Ivy Oooh—d'you remember lipstick?

Jacintha Oh, and plucked eyebrows.

Arnold Silence. There's nature to beat.

Mrs Buller It's chaos out here, if you don't watch it. Cows bursting, hens migrating—it's not just jam sandwiches and the odd ant.

Mr Smith Into line, Mrs Buller.

Mrs Buller Are you talking to me?

Mr Smith Yes, I'm giving orders. The country air has done me a power of good and made me feel ridiculously self-confident. Jacintha, mow the big meadow.

Jacintha Oh.

Mr Smith Ivy, clean out the stables.

Ivy Oh.

Mr Smith Beauty, churn the butter.

Beauty Done.

Mr Smith Then chop the logs.

Beauty Done.

Mr Smith Then mow the medium meadow, the small meadow and the very long meadow.

Beauty Done, done, done.

Mr Smith I knew it.

Beauty What else is there?

Mrs Buller Oh listen to her! Isn't she marvellous? If she goes on at this rate she'll be just like me.
Beauty Not quite, Mrs Buller. I'm beautiful.
Jacintha And an absolute little creep.
Mrs Buller Who said that? Own up.
Mr Smith Now, now, Mrs Buller, stop that.
Mrs Buller Are you talking to me again?
Mr Smith Yes. I feel so ridiculously self-confident I'm going to have another go at life. I shall leave you all here and see if I can make a fortune again in the city.
Beauty Oh Papa, how wonderful!
Mrs Buller It isn't wonderful. It's stupid.
Mr Smith I made a fortune once, I might do it again.
Mrs Buller Never.
Ivy Yes, he might. You go to the city, Father, and bring us lots of lovely presents to make up for this awful year we've spent in slavery to growth. Some new dresses.
Jacintha Some new hats.
Ivy Some new shoes.
Arnold Some elbow grease.
Mr Smith And you Beauty, what do you want?
Beauty Well, nothing, really.
Jacintha Oh, typical.
Ivy Goody, goody, goody.
Beauty But I really don't want anything, except for him to come back safe and sound.
Ivy You're a real pain.
Mrs Buller D'you want to have to kiss me, do you? D'you want to have to come and do back scrubbing duty in the bath tonight? D'you want to have to trim my corns and put mustard plasters on?
Ivy
Jacintha } (*together*) No.
Mrs Buller Then you treat your sister as she deserves and when your father's gone on this fool's errand, you can swill out the pigs.
Mr Smith Beauty, I must bring you something back.
Beauty Well, a rose, then, bring me a rose. There aren't any here and I love them.
Mrs Buller Nice, sensible and cheap. Arnold, where's the boss's bicycle?

Arnold exits and brings on a penny-farthing

Mrs Buller Good. Get off and get back so we can get on with the serious business of keeping the countryside under control.
Beauty Goodbye, Papa! Be careful of the Doom Laden Woods.
All Goodbye!

Mr Smith exits on the bicycle

Mrs Buller And back to work, you droopy draws, you.

USER 104: Fx: Gaia '99

MULTI 047: Harp

SCENE 5

A forest grove. Frontcloth

Candy and Snowdrop enter, Snowdrop leading

Storm noises

Candy Why d'you want a storm?
Snowdrop Just shut up and listen.
Candy Snowdrop, I've been a good fairy for very much longer than most
    people and that is no way to speak——
Snowdrop Look, here he comes, Mr Smith, back from the city, made
    another mess of it, like Mrs Buller said he would. Just his bicycle, all
    depressed and sad. (*She produces more storm or thunder*)
Candy He doesn't need a storm, he needs comfort.
Snowdrop He needs to feel cold and hungry. He's near the castle.

More storm

Candy Oh, he's near the castle. Very clever.
Snowdrop Sh.
Candy Snowdrop?

Mr Smith enters on his bicycle, very depressed

Mr Smith Failed again. Absolutely broke. And as if that weren't enough,
    I'm cold and hungry as well.
Candy We need a bicycle spell here.

Song 6: The Bicycle Spell (*sung as often as desired*)

(*Singing*)   Bicycle, bicycle, gentle and magical,
              Go to the castle so lonely and tragical.
              Open the way for the good and the beautiful,
              Bicycle, bicycle do what is dutiful.

The bicycle moves on its own through the trees

Mr Smith What's happening? I can't even steer a bicycle anymore.

Candy and Snowdrop exit, as the frontcloth rises on . . .

SCENE 6

The courtyard of the Beast's Castle

*The Bicycle Song continues as Mr Smith arrives here. The sound of a low
growl joins it. Both fade as the weather becomes sunny and pleasant*

*At the back of the courtyard is a door where the Beast is waiting unseen. There
is a grille in the door and at certain times the eyes of the Beast glow there.
There are roses growing in the courtyard*

The bicycle halts with the surprised Mr Smith

Mr Smith Good heavens. Where am I? (*He dismounts*) It's warm, anyway,
and comfy, sort of. (*He looks round at things*)

*A table and chair appear. There is a meal on the table. After a second or two,
Mr Smith sees the table and the food*

Goodness, food. (*He looks round*) I wonder ... (*He puts his finger in and
tastes the food*) Oooh, wonderful. (*He looks round again*) I'd better wait,
just in case it's someone else's. Isn't it all nice though? Roses, peace, lovely
weather. (*He looks at the food again*) There is only one chair. I wonder if it
is for me?

Wine suddenly appears

Oh! (*Calling*) I'm awfully thirsty, whoever you are. Would you mind if I
had a drink?

Nothing

Well, here goes. (*He drinks*) Nobody seems to mind. (*He sits*) In which
case, I think this must be for me too. The person who owns this place
must be a magician.

*As he eats the eyes of the Beast slowly glow. Mr Smith never sees them. It is
possible the children will call out, in which case he must look and the eyes must
go out. This business can be plotted as required*

(*Calling to the castle*) This food's really marvellous. I'm really very
grateful. You're very kind whoever you are. Must've known how hungry
and miserable I was. (*He gets up. Still to the castle*) I think I'd better be
going to face the family with the bad news that I'm just as incompetent as
ever. Of course, I was going to take them presents, dresses and things—
and my Beauty wanted a rose. (*He looks at the roses. Then to the audience*)
I'm sure nobody would notice if I just cut one. I mean, whoever it is lives
here must be ever so rich and they wouldn't miss one rose. (*He crosses to
the roses*) I know the meal was meant to be eaten, and the roses are meant
to stay growing on their stalks—but it's just for my Beauty, who works so
hard and asks for so little. I'll take one anyway. (*He takes one rose guiltily
and hides it with his hand*)

*There is a terrific roar. The Beast smashes down the door and appears etched
in strong light from above and behind. He is truly terrible to look at, half bird,
half lion, much of him scaly and his feet like a great hen's. The noise is awful*

Beast (*thunderous*) You fiend! You stole one of my living roses! I gave you
comfort, I gave you food and warmth and now you steal one of my living
roses!
Mr Smith (*on his knees*) My lord, take it back.
Beast (*knocking it from his hand*) It's dying. You cut it off and it's dying.
Roses are the only beautiful things I have. (*He smashes the things on the
table*)

Mr Smith My lord——

Beast Don't flatter me. I'm not "my lord"! I'm the Beast! (*He smashes the chair*) I long to do lovely things like giving people hot dinners, but every time I try—people turn horrid.

Mr Smith Do you have many guests, then?

Beast Of course not! You're the first.

Mr Smith Then——

Beast Don't argue! Say your prayers, rose killer, because I'm going to do what beasts are meant to do and kill you.

Mr Smith No!

Beast Yes.

Mr Smith Oh Beast—the rose was for my daughter. She's so kind—all my daughters are—well, some more than others—and I wanted to give her what she asked for. I like giving too, you see, rather too much, probably, but the point is——

Beast So, you like giving, do you. In that case, I'll let you go if you will give me one of your daughters in exchange for yourself.

Mr Smith Oh!

Beast No—one of them must give herself willingly, willingly do you hear, willingly to die instead of you.

Mr Smith No!

Beast And if she doesn't then you must come back and meet your fate.

Mr Smith But I can't ask one of my daughters to do that.

Beast Yes, you can! We'll see then if your family loves you. ~~And you can take a chest of rubbishy goodies in case they don't. Something for them to live off if I have to kill you.~~

A ~~chest appears~~

~~**Mr Smith** How thought~~ful.

Beast Now go. Bicycle, take this miserable rose-killing little man away.

The bicycle moves on its own

Go on, go!

Mr Smith Yes, Beast, certainly, Beast.

Beast And say thank you.

Mr Smith Thank you.

Mr Smith leaves

The Beast howls horribly

Beast Why does everything get spoilt? It always does. And I go on here on my own, with nothing to do but get angry, angry, angry! (*He howls appallingly and stamps around*)

MR SMITH: You're very hard.
BEAST: As nails! But I will do this, I will send them all a chest of rubbishy goodies. Something for them to live off if I have to kill you.
(A CHEST APPEARS)
MR SMITH Well, that is thoughtful (ATTACHES CHEST TO BIKE)

SCENE 7

A frontcloth

Candy and Snowdrop enter

Candy Do you think you've been entirely wise, my dear?

Snowdrop We're in this together, aren't we?

Candy I'm just your tutor, and frankly he's more revolting than I thought possible.

Snowdrop We have to go on, Candy.

Candy And I didn't expect such a temper. I wonder what school he went to.

Dolores appears with her hammock

Dolores He's going to murder someone before long. Then there'll be the whole guilt thing, and he'll be even more lonely, and even more angry — oh lovely.

Snowdrop Candy and I know there's something we can do for him, don't we.

Dolores He's lost in a permanent rage, like all the poor fools who refuse to marry me.

Snowdrop I won't believe that, and nor will Candy, Candy?

Song 7: He's Gone Down the Drain in a Rage

Dolores

He's —
Sad, sad,
A lout of a lad,
Furious frantic,
Frustrated and mad,
Nothing can change him,
He's barnstorming bad,
And he's gone down the drain in a rage.

Sob, sob,
A scab of a slob,
I've made a nobody
Out of a nob,
A peach of a prince
To a plonking great yob
Who's gone down the drain in a rage.

POSSIBLE/CHANGE:-
Sob, sob,
A gem of a job,
I've turned a somebody
Into a slob.

He's carping all day for a kick-off,
And seething all over the shop.
The teeniest tut, or a tick-off
And whoops with a whoosh
He goes over the top.

Whang, clang
He goes with a bang

Fearless and foaming
He flashes his fang.
Ever in bovver
He don't give a hang
'Cos he's gone down the drain in a rage.

Snowdrop I'll try
You to defy
Making your monster
The tweetiest pie
I'll bring him round
To a regular guy
A joyful and jovial gent.

Candy True blue
All the way through
Mending his manners
Will make him anew.

Candy } Also we'll bring him
Snowdrop } A girl he can woo,
This joyful and jovial gent.

Dolores His temper is terribly quick up,
If things aren't as clear as a bell.
The hint of a hurdle or hiccup
He loses his head and the rest goes as well.

All Ding, dong,
Once he goes wrong
Howls like a banshee
And bangs like a gong.
Then in a trice
He's a match for King Kong
As he goes down the drain,
It's the plug hole again,
As he goes down the drain in a rage.

Snowdrop Well, it's too late to worry now we've set it going.
Candy You've set it going, to be precise.
Dolores And it's going wrong. (*She laughs*)

SCENE 8   Sit com syn

The little place in the country

Ivy and Jacintha are busy unpacking all sorts of things from the chest. Arnold is looking sadly on. Mrs Buller and Beauty are comforting poor old Mr Smith

Beauty Papa, Papa, don't cry.
Mr Smith I can't help it.
Mrs Buller You must help it. Tears upset everyone. Everyone. (*In tears herself*)

Arnold (*his arm around her*) There, there, poor old thing.

Ivy It's all very well for you to talk, Beauty. If you'd been a normal, selfish greedy little pig like the rest of us he wouldn't have gone looking for roses at all, would he? (*To Jacintha*) Here, try this tutu.

Jacintha Not my colour.

Beauty It is all my fault, then?

Mr Smith No! It was mine, going off to seek my fortune. I was consumed with dreams of better things.

Mrs Buller Dreams always lead to chaos. I know, I've had them.

Jacintha So who's going to go back in his place?

Arnold (*looking at Ivy*) Yes who?

Ivy Not me, not with all this lovely stuff.

Mr Smith I'll go back myself. I'm an old man with not long to live.

Jacintha And you cost quite a lot to keep.

Ivy Quite a chance for him, really, to lay down his life for his daughters like a good father should. Oh, look at this. Money.

Mrs Buller You mean you'd let your father die for a handful of trinkets?

Jacintha (*putting another bag of gold in Mrs Buller's hand*) Try that for trinkets. We're rich again, so keep quiet and do what you're told.

Mrs Buller You—it's—I've never heard of such cheek. (*She throws the gold away*)

Ivy You go, Arnold, go on.

Arnold Me?

Ivy Get yourself a hayfork and go and give him a good old prod. Be a hero.

Arnold But I'm a coward. Mr Smith, I don't want to be a hero. I want to be a coward for ever and ever.

Mr Smith It wouldn't do any good. The Beast would kill him straight off. He'll kill us all straight off if we don't do as he says.

Mrs Buller Exactly. A bargain has been made and it must be kept.

Ivy You keep it then. Put on this tutu and he'll swallow you in half a second. No-one else wants it.

Mrs Buller Don't you see? Your father has given his word and it must be kept.

Beauty Yes. So, Papa, I'll go. It was all my fault.

Arnold No.

Mrs Buller You're not to say that.

Beauty I want to go. I want to save his life.

Ivy (*still at the chest*) Good, it settles everything.

Mr Smith It must be me.

Beauty But it would break my heart to lose the person I love most in all the world. And even if you do go, I'll go too, because if you were killed I wouldn't want to live.

Mrs Buller (*much moved*) Oh, Arnold.

Arnold Hanky?

Beauty So since I asked for the rose, and he wants one of your daughters, it has to be me. Doesn't it, Mrs Buller?

Mrs Buller Oh blast it! Blast it, yes it does.

Mr Smith You mean you can't think of a way out?

Mrs Buller I've tried and tried.

Arnold Then try harder.

Mrs Buller I can't. He gave his word, and you have to keep your word in this world, or chaos follows.

Arnold But it's Beauty.

Mrs Buller I know, but it's an enormous sacrifice and that's always good for people.

Arnold Not for her it's not.

Mrs Buller Well it can't be helped and do your shoe-laces up.

Ivy Who left that money lying around? (*She moves to retrieve what Mrs Buller threw away*)

Mrs Buller Your sister is going to her death and you're chasing money?

Ivy sighs and turns round and comes back empty-handed

Beauty Goodbye, then, Papa.

Mr Smith Oh, my goodness gracious.

They hug. Jacintha takes out onions

Jacintha Better look sad. Though actually it suits us rather well, no more goody goody making us look selfish. Have an onion. (*Cut onion?*)

Beauty Goodbye, Mrs Buller. Let me give you a kiss.

Mrs Buller You don't have to. Though it is your last chance.

They kiss

Beauty Goodbye, both of you.

Ivy (*crying with the onion*) I'm ever so overcome; aren't you, Jacintha? Completely overcome.

Jacintha (*crying*) Terribly overcome. As overcome as anything.

Jacintha }
Ivy   (*together*) Booohhoo.

Beauty Goodbye, Arnold, don't cry, just go and get the bicycle. It knows the way, I think.

A tearful Arnold goes off. He returns with the bicycle during the next

Mr Smith Mind of its own, that bicycle. I don't know how it manages it.

Mrs Buller And remember, dearest girl, that whatever happens, we're all thinking of you, and we're proud, very proud, that in the face of absolute chaos, you kept your father's bargain.

Song 8: Though Dead I Kept My Word

(*Singing*) Though the way looks uninviting
And the future's insecure
And you know they've got your number
And you won't see your dad no more
There's one great light a-shining,
One chorus to be heard.
'Tis the cherubs who sing in praise of you
"Though dead, she kept her word".

Mrs Buller   When the Beast drips with saliva
(*with*   And his eyes have a ghastly flame,
backing)   And his claws begin to itch for
                His blood-thirsty little game,
                Then raise your eyes to heaven
                And trill like a mocking bird,
                "At the close of play I am glad to say
                Though dead, I kept my word."

                When the cattle low in the twilight
                And the hens do their evening lay,
                And the world snores comfily onwards
                Through to a bright new day,
                And there you lie dismembered
                And probably half-interred,
                To the rising sun we will cry "Well, done!
                Though dead, she kept—
                While others slept—
                Though dead she kept her word!"

All Goodbye, goodbye!

Beauty and the bicycle go

Jacintha picks up the bag of money that is still lying about. Ivy sees her

Ivy Jacintha, that's mine. Jacintha!

SCENE 9

A frontcloth

A nail-biting Snowdrop alone

Snowdrop (*to the audience*) There you are you see, I've got Beauty off to the castle. But, the trouble is, the Beast has no idea about entertaining girls, and she's so honest, she'll say something straightaway about how draughty the place is, or how she doesn't like the decoration, not having any music—I know he'd magic it all up if he thought about it—he's got a heart of gold—I have to believe that—but if she says things he doesn't like, well, whoosh. King Kong time, like we said. I know. Let's call out and tell him what she would like. Then he'd know and get it for her. Come on. Loud. What would she like?

Kids call out things. If they suggest TV Snowdrop says

There isn't any television here. But she might like a magic mirror so she can see what's going on at home. A magic mirror.

Various things will continue to be suggested, and then:

Well that should help. Let's see how it goes. Candy? It's going to be all right.
Candy (*off*) I hope so.

SCENE 10

The Courtyard of the Beast's Castle

There is a place laid at the table, there are lovely lights, there is a harpsichord, a large mirror and presents

Beauty enters on her bicycle. She gets off

Beauty Well, it looks lovely. I'd no idea it would be so pretty. (*Seeing the harpsichord*) Oh, a harpsichord, just like home. And a whole shelf full of books and presents. Surely if he's given me all this he doesn't want to kill me straight away. ~~And roses, look. I suppose these are the roses that Papa picked for me.~~

The harpsichord starts to play the "Rose is a Rose" song from earlier in the act

Oh! The song I was learning to play when we were rich! I wish I were at home now. I'd love to see poor Papa and know what he's doing.

The mirror glows and behind it we see Mr Smith and Mrs Buller crying

Mrs Buller Keep a stiff upper lip, Mr Smith. Once you let go of your feelings there's chaos all over everything. And you two stop laughing.
Mr Smith They're trying to cheer me up.
Mrs Buller They're completely out of hand.

Ivy and Jacintha flounce into view

Jacintha We'll have a few balls and choose a few husbands.
Ivy And live on chocolate creams.
Jacintha Coffee creams.
Ivy Chocolate creams.
Mrs Buller Silence! Who's going to get the crops in?
Jacintha We don't need to anymore.
Ivy We're rich again.
Mr Smith I wish we weren't.

The picture fades

Beauty Papa! Oh! I wish I could touch him. I shall never be used to being away from him.

The sounds of the Beast arriving. A sort of anxious sighing

Oh, this must be the Beast. I really am going to meet my fate, so I must be tremendously brave.

The Beast enters

She looks at him, is startled by his awful looks and looks away. He on the other hand is impressed by her beauty. Finally

Beast Good-evening. They call me the Beast.
Beauty Good-evening. They call me Beauty.
Beast I'm not surprised.
Beauty I'm not surprised they call you the Beast. I'm famous for being truthful.
Beast Then did you come here willingly? No-one forced you?
Beauty No-one forced me.
Beast You are a very good daughter, and I am happily surprised. Will you sit down?

She does so. Food appears

Beauty Oh! Did you do that?
Beast I get whatever I want, except company. May I watch you eat?
Beauty If you like.
Beast I'm very ugly so if you want me to go I will.
Beauty You are even uglier than Mrs Buller, our housekeeper, as a matter of fact, but I think you must be quite kind so I'd like you to stay.
Beast I'm also extremely stupid.

Beauty laughs

   (*A bit dangerous*) Are you laughing at me?
Beauty Oh no. Only clever people say they're stupid because they know how hard it is to be really clever. I think you must be really clever, in spite of looking like that.
Beast Oh!
Beauty There are lots of people in the world who look ever so nice but are in fact quite nasty.
Beast (*over-excited*) Oh yes! Your father for example. He wasn't above pinching my roses was he, and causing them to die and your sisters, you saw them in the mirror—I know how treacherous human beings can be. (*He snaps a soup spoon in anger*)
Beauty My sisters have been a little spoilt that's their trouble.
Beast Well I've not been spoilt at all and that's mine! You ought to know I've fallen in love with you. Will you marry me?
Beauty Aren't you going to kill me?
Beast No.
Beauty I think I'd rather you did.
Beast Why?
Beauty (*to the audience*) Oh dear. I didn't expect this. Well, I've always told the truth . . .
Beast Tell me if you will marry me.
Beauty No, Beast, I can't marry you. You're just too ugly for words.

The Beast smashes a chair in frustration ——— *happy crush*

Beast (*crying*) Aaah! Aaah! I knew it, I am truly, truly appalling.
Beauty But you do seem to be nice.

Beast Nice isn't enough. I must tell you, I won't give up asking even though
I know you are going to keep on turning me down.
Beauty I wish you wouldn't.
Beast And I'll improve myself you see. I'll improve.

Song 9: I'll Somehow Shine

(*Singing*)   I'll somehow shine
                 With glitter and with glory
                 I'll brush my teeth
                 So you don't fear my breath.
                 I'll bathe my eyes
                 So they're not veined and gory
                 I'll smile so I
                 Won't scare you half to death.

                 I'll learn to walk
                 On eggshells and not crack them
                 I'll learn to talk
                 Like any sucking dove
                 If people laugh
                 At me I won't attack them
                 And most of all
                 I'll learn to speak of love.

                 I will improve
                 My powers of concentration
                 And read long books
                 Like nicely spoken folks
                 I will be brilliant
                 In my conversation
                 Be famous for
                 My clever little jokes.

Beast   I'll move the earth
(*with chorus*   To show you what I'm made of.
backing)   I'll bare my soul
                 To all the skies above.
                 I'll rid my flesh
                 Of all that you're afraid of
                 And most of all
                 I'll learn to speak of love.
                 And most of all
                 I'll learn to speak of love.

*Throughout this he occasionally breaks things or bends them. As he finishes
he staggers through a doorway and smashes it. Pieces fall*

Beauty hears, scared

*Dolores appears on top of something, smiling. Snowdrop and Candy appear
and look hot and bothered*

Beauty He's so ugly.
Dolores And he's mine.
Beauty He's so ugly, ugly, ugly, and I'm alone with him for ever.
Candy (*to the audience*) Just go and have an ice-cream while we think. All
   right?

CURTAIN

ACT II

A flash. Dolores is in her hammock drinking gin

Dolores She won't ever marry him. She won't because he's ugly, and ugly things are ever so yuk. Fun of course, but yuk. As you'll find out, I'm happy to say, because some of that ice-cream you had in the interval was laced with Yuk Potion Mark Two, so one or two of you may start looking a bit peculiar soon. Did any of the adults have the bitter from the bar? You did? Oh dear oh dear, well, I'm afraid to say that before we get to the end of the story—and it's going to be my end, not Cowslip and Candy's— one or two people here will be so yuk that no-one will love them at all. In fact, given half a chance, I might get the whole lot of you turning yuk, and I'll put you all into lonely castles, you horrible set of Nicies, you. Meanwhile, good old selfish Ivy and Jacintha, rich as anything because of the money the Beast sent them, they are getting married to Sir Simon and Sir Thomas. Just as it should be. Two proper, thoroughly self-interested weddings.

She chuckles. The sound of wedding bells

SCENE 1

The Smiths' home again, now looking very prosperous and ready for a wedding reception

Present are Ivy and Jacintha in wedding gear and Sir Simon and Sir Thomas, and Mr Smith and Mrs Buller and Arnold. The bells ring out and confetti falls. A slightly stately wedding march tune plays. Throughout the song, Ivy, Jacintha, Sir Simon and Sir Thomas have false smiles

Song 10: Now We're Hitched

Ivy **Jacintha**	Now we're hitched, Thought that we were ditched. Though they're pretty crummy They are male.
Sir Simon **Sir Thomas**	Pressed our suit Once they'd got the loot, Though they're sour and scummy, Flat and stale.

Ivy	Mine thinks he's The bee's bewitching knees.
Jacintha	This one thinks he's witty And he's not.
Sir Simon	Mine's no belle Moans away like hell.
Sir Simon **Sir Thomas** }	And neither smells too pretty When they're hot.

Chorus

All	But we're married and it's blissful Pearls and diamonds by the fistful. Shut your eyes and think they're kissful, That's the way.
	And we mutter as we mingle And we hear the coffers jingle, That we're better wed than single Any day.
Ivy **Jacintha** }	Though we've got Really quite a lot; Rubies on our fingers— Thrilled to bits
	Still we've two Carbuncles to woo And the knowledge lingers They are twits.
Sir Simon **Sir Thomas** }	Though we smile, We led down the aisle A pair of horse-hair sofas For our wives.
	Once we've ceased Eating at this feast We're stuck with the left-overs All our lives.

Chorus

All	But we're married and it's blissful Pearls and diamonds by the fistful. Shut your eyes and think they're kissful, That's the way.
	And we mutter as we mingle And we hear the coffers jingle, That we're better wed than single Any day.

Mrs Buller Now then! This is the happiest day of your lives, so jump to it.
Laugh!

[Handwritten annotations:]

MR S. Not much cheer.
Beauty isn't here,
Dead & buried, off in somewhere
bleak.
Old & ill
I believe I will
Be cooped up in my coffin
in a week.

ARNOLD You did that,
Ridiculous old bat.
But for you She could be
fighting fit.

MRS B. She did right,
Dying in the night,
But, though it's as it should
be, I could spit.

Jacintha What on earth are the rest going to be like?

Mr Smith Well, I'm not happy at all and I never will be again.

Mrs Buller Just let bygones be bygones and have a ham sandwich.

Mr Smith I can't put anything in my mouth without thinking of my daughter being devoured. A seat! (*He has a collapsing fit*)

Arnold (*to Mrs Buller*) You did this.

Mrs Buller I did not.

Sir Simon Oh dear, Mr Smith. You do look poorly. Have you made your will?

Ivy I'm the oldest, Father, so you've left everything to me I hope.

Jacintha No, he's left everything to me because I'm the most beautiful.

Sir Thomas The least ugly.

Mrs Buller Let this be understood. The old devil is not going to die because I'm here to give him strength and comfort and if he tries dying, I'll kick him. Now get this inside you and don't drop any crumbs. (*She forces a sandwich on him*)

Sir Thomas Well, I hope he leaves me more than just the doormat.

Jacintha What doormat?

Sir Thomas You, my love. Scrubby, tattered and in need of a jolly good wash. Ha, ha, ha. I'm the witty one.

A boot from Ivy

Oooh!

Sir Simon I hope he leaves me enough to have my hair permed every day.

Ivy What about my hair?

Sir Simon Have you got any? Ooh! Ooh! Down, Rover.

Mr Smith Stop! You're married and you mustn't argue. It's bad for your faces.

Ivy Nothing could be bad for my Simon's face. It's like fresh butter, isn't it dear, needs slapping about a bit. (*She slaps it about a bit*)

Sir Simon Ouch! Ouch! Ouch! Come on, Tommy. Let's go and play French Cricket.

Sir Thomas Ooh! French Cricket!

Ivy In that case, we'll go and have Women's Talk.

Jacintha And we'll say how horrid our husbands are behind their backs.

All put their tongues out at one another and leave

Mr Smith Has it come to this so soon?

Arnold Yes, it has. The good gone, the bad worse, chaos.

Mrs Buller There's no chaos about when I'm here.

Arnold You brought this chaos.

Mrs Buller It was him stealing roses.

Arnold It was you.

Mrs Buller It was him!

Mr Smith Quiet! I just want to be a happy old-age pensioner with a very sweet cup of cocoa.

Arnold I'll get it for you.

Mrs Buller He doesn't want cocoa. He wants fresh air. Come on, be a brave old man and smile.

Mr Smith Smile? I don't know where the muscles are.

Mrs Buller (*pulling him up*) Up you get. Out you go. It's all an attitude of mind.

Arnold Careful you don't break him.

Mrs Buller He needs to pull his socks up. He's got a lot of life to live yet.

Arnold That's true, you have, Mr Smith.

Mr Smith I don't want it.

They are now at the front of the stage

SCENE 2

Mrs Buller, Arnold and Mr Smith in front of the cloth

Song 11: Pull Your Socks Up

Mrs Buller	When the world is very drear,
	Like an ageing glass of beer
	And you'd rather you weren't here,
	Pull your socks up.
Arnold	If another fellow's kissed
	The best girl upon your list
	And your knickers are a-twist,
	Pull your socks up.
Mrs Buller	If you're dying for a chew
	Of a lovely lump of stew
	And your false teeth won't undo,
	Pull your socks up.
Arnold	If your bike has turned to rust,
	Or your piggy bank has bust
	And you've lost a fiver, just
	Pull your socks up.

Chorus

All (*with reluctant Mr Smith*)	Pull your socks up,
	Pull your socks up,
	Even though your life appears to be a box up.
Arnold } **Mrs Buller** }	If your favourite daughter's ~~dead~~ *gone*
	And ~~there's only us instead,~~ *you have to carry on,*
	Pull your socks,
	Pull your socks,
	Pull your socks up.
Mr Smith (*resistant to cheer*)	If you feel the urge to moan,
	Give a grunt or two and groan,
	And you'd rather be alone,

Arnold **Mrs Buller** }	Pull your socks up.
Arnold	If it's raining and you're weak, And in what appears like pique Your umbrella starts to leak,
Arnold **Mrs Buller** }	Pull your socks up.
Mr Smith (*as before*)	If you're walking just as if You could walk over a cliff 'Cos you'd rather be a stiff,
Arnold **Mrs Buller** }	Pull your socks up.
Mrs Buller	If you're gazing at the sky When a birdie from on high Drops a greeting in your eye,
Arnold **Mrs Buller** }	Pull your socks up.

Chorus (sung as before)

All	Pull your socks up, Pull your socks up, Even though your life appears to be a box up. If you're bothersome and blue And there's nothing else to do, Pull your socks, Pull your socks, Pull your socks up.
Mr Smith	Not down or sideways,
All	Pull your socks, Pull your socks, Pull your socks up. Right up!

Mr Smith (*speaking*) Well, I'll do what I can, but you might as well know, I am not long for this world.

Mrs Buller
Arnold } (*together*) Oh yes you are!

Mr Smith (*quiet and determined*) Oh—no—I'm—not.

SCENE 3

The Beast's Castle Courtyard

Beauty has been looking in the big mirror and the Beast is standing behind her

Beauty Oh poor Papa. He looks so ill. And it'll be worse now Ivy and Jacintha have left home.

Beast That wouldn't make me ill. They're horrid, absolutely, impossibly, revoltingly, downright horrid and mean and they tell lies and don't care about you, or your poor old father, who kills roses but is nice, and if I had my way, I'd tear them into very small bits and post them down the drain! And I'd spit, oh yes, you should see me spit! I'd like to spit on those two awful baggages until they melted, or got so stuck in the goo and gum and mess that they were like two wasps in a jam-jar! There! If I meet them, I'll spit on them, that's what I'll do, I'll spit until I've no spit left! And I've a lot of spit, I can tell you! When I'm roused, I'm all spit, and when I spit on them, they'll look like two great spit balls so you can't tell there was ever anything human there at all! Nothing but spit, that's what there'd be! Spit! Just spit, spit, spit! Spit!

Beauty That wasn't very nice.

Beast No, but I am getting better at keeping my temper, aren't I?

Beauty Are you?

Beast Yes. But when I think of those two appalling great lumps of——

Beauty Beast, you've been so kind to me while I've been here——

Beast Yes.

Beauty So I've a favour to ask of you I'm sure you'll grant.

Beast Will you marry me?

Beauty Oh, do stop asking that. I do *like* you, but you know I'll never love you. We're just friends that's all.

Beast Just promise you won't ever leave me, then.

Beauty I have done. But—now keep calm—there's a good Beast—Papa is so unhappy that I think he's dying.

Beast Well, he's old.

Beauty He's only fifty-six, actually, but life hasn't treated him kindly. Now, of course I'll stay here with you, but I would like to go and see Papa, just once, to show him I'm all right. If I don't I might die myself, and you wouldn't like that, would you?

Beast I wouldn't have you suffer any pain at all.

Beauty Oh, you kind old monster.

Beast You go to him, then, and I'll just stay here and die of a broken heart.

Beauty Oh don't make such a thing about it. I only want to go for a week.

Beast A week?

Beauty Yes.

Beast Then, if you promise to come back in a week, I don't mind.

Beauty You're the best friend I ever had. I'll come back in a week, I promise you.

Beast You promise?

Beauty I promise.

Song 12: In a Week

(*Singing*)   In a week
            I'll be back and being friends
            In just a week
            After visiting Papa
            To show him just how good you are
            Without a single scar

	Or toothmark on my cheek.
Beast	Seven days,
	You'll be back to make amends
	In seven days.
	We will babble here again
	About the funny ways of men
	I'll bring you lovely food again
	And gaze and gaze,
	In seven days.
Beauty	I'll play
	Upon the harpsichord all day.
Beast	And then you'll sing
	About the lovely things of spring,
Beauty ⎫	And then we'll talk the way we do
Beast ⎰	Prattle on the whole night through
	And then catch our death of cold
	By walking bare foot through the dew.
Beast	For a week,
	I'll be counting every day
	For just a week,
	And to help to pass the time
	I shall attempt to be sublime
	I'll rub and scrub till I'm
	All exquisite and sleek.
Beauty	Seven days
	With my friends to laugh and play
	For seven days!
	I'll run up and down the stairs
	I'll go to shops and visit fairs,
	I'll cuddle teddy bears
	And life will be ablaze!
	In seven days.
Beauty ⎫	Of course,
Beast ⎰	There will be moments of remorse
	When we're alone,
	And the other's on their own.
	But we're not the sort to moon,
	And we'll know pretty soon
	We'll be chattering like monkeys.
	Morning, night and afternoon.

In a week, (just a week)
We'll be floating like a feather
In a week,
And it will not matter whether
Time has dragged we'll be together
In a week, a single week, just a week,
A little week.

DOLORES   Sleep sweetly and dream
Of living a life that's a treat
With parties galore
Where your friends from next door
All come to play out in the street.

Dream, little one, dream,
Say farewell to trouble and strife,
There's more than just toys
Waiting for you, there's boys
And a wonderful whale of a life.

Candy and Snowdrop enter singing

CANDY) _ Dream, little one, dream	DOLORES	Oh Lord.
SNOWDROP) Dream of the one you have left.		Give over.

Think of his mind,
How he's good and he's kind
So don't leave him sad and   Live in clover
           bereft.

CANDY   ) _ Sleep sweetly and dream
SNOWDROP) And don't leave your promise undone
DOLORES   You gibe and you give.
Kick the habit and live
And look after number one.

DOLORES	Dream, little one, dream,	SNOWDROP
	Of choccies and ciggies and drink.	She'll be plastered!
CANDY	Work hard and play,	
	But don't lose your way.	
DOLORES	Losing ways is more fun than you think.	
		CANDY It's disaster!

Snowdrop Candy. Beauty's gone home!

Candy And these good people are going to the dogs, so my first duty is to them.

Snowdrop But nothing'll work if she goes home and stays there, and I know Dolores is trying to work her wicked will on her.

Candy The muddles you get with apprentices. All right. I'll be back to help you (*the audience*) in a minute, so keep calm while we see what that sodden old ruin's up to up here. We'll hide, Snowdrop. When in doubt always hide, that's my advice to you. Come on, get that cloth up.

They leave the stage as . . .

The curtain goes up to reveal Beauty asleep in bed in no particular place with Dolores standing over her

Song 13: Sleep Sweetly and Dream (A Lullaby)

Dolores   Sleep sweetly and dream
            Of living a life that's a treat
            With parties galore
            Where your friends from next door
            All come to play out in the street.

            Dream, little one, dream,
            Say farewell to trouble and strife,
            There's more than just toys
            Waiting for you, there's boys
            And a wonderful whale of a life.

Candy and Snowdrop enter singing

Candy   ⎧ Dream, little one, dream
Snowdrop ⎩ Dream of the one you have   **Dolores** Oh Lord.
                 left.   Give over.
             Think of his mind;
             How he's good and he's kind
             So don't leave him sad and
                 bereft. *   Live in clover!

Dolores   Dream, little one, dream,   of delights
             And don't leave your
                 promise undone.
             You give and you give —
Dolores Kick the habit and live,
             And look after number one.

Candy
Snowdrop ⎱ Sleep sweetly and dream

             Of duty much more than of fun.
Dolores   Give up love, give up church, ·
             Leave your friend in the lurch —

Beast (*speaking*)   Go to bed now, my dear, and in the morning you'll wake up at home. When you want to come back here, look in this little hand mirror.

Magically it appears and he gives it to her

It will bring you back by magic.
Beauty Thank you.
Beast You'll have to want to look in it, of course. I can't force you. Ever.
Beauty I'll go to bed now and fall asleep as quickly as possible. Goodbye. I'll see you in a week's time.

She goes

Beast Now. Beautiful and sleek. (*He sits before the mirror*) First my scales. (*He starts to polish furiously*) Come on, shine. Shine! They won't do it! Aaah! My hair then. Comb. Comb!

One appears in his hand

Now, lovely locks, come on, lovely locks. (*He combs furiously*) Aaah, it hurts. (*He looks in the mirror*) Ridiculous. It looks ridiculous!

It does

Perhaps a garland of roses?

One drops round his neck. He gazes in the mirror

How can she ever love something like that, except as a sort of pet? Even if she comes back, which she probably won't.

Song 12a: In a Week (Reprise)

(*Singing*)   In a week,
            She will pamper me and pet me
            In a week.
            But the thought that does upset me
            Is that Beauty might forget me
            And it leaves me so that I can hardly speak.
            In fact it makes me just a little weak.

He sits gazing mournfully at himself

SCENE 4

The frontcloth

Candy appears in the audience and Snowdrop a little later on the stage

Candy Oh heavens! Some of you look dreadful. That Dolores woman's been at it again, hasn't she? Hasn't she? Given you some Yuk Potion? Was it the ice-cream in the interval? Yes, right, exactly. I should've known. Oh, the poor gallery.

CANDY) _	Sleep sweetly and dream
SNOWDROP)	Of duty much more than of fun.
DOLORES	Give up love, give up church,
	Leave your friend in the lurch
	And look after number one.

CANDY Give up church?
     Whatever will she
     say next?

CANDY) _	Sleep sweetly and dream
SNOWDROP)	And don't leave your promise undone
DOLORES	You give and you give.
	Kick the habit and live
	And look after number one.

	Don't think of number -
ALL)	Don't think of) _ number one.
DOLORES)	Look after)

The music stops

Candy (*speaking*) Give up church? Whatever will she say next?

The music starts again

Dolores   And look after number one.
Candy
Snowdrop }   Don't think of number—
All   Look after (Don't think of) number one!

Dolores I've won. You can buzz off, Dandelion.
Snowdrop But——
Dolores And as for you lot (*the audience*) I'm working on Yuk Potion Mark Three, which turns you nasty a good deal quicker than Mark Two seems to be doing.

She laughs and leaves

Candy I'd better go and find something a bit stronger than the last spell. Just keep your heads.
Snowdrop What about getting Beauty to save the Beast?
Candy We've done everything we can about that. Really, you're an absolute menace sometimes.

She leaves

Snowdrop But don't you *see*? We can't save *them* without beating Dolores. (*To the audience*) Really, she's putting you in terrible danger. (*She starts to go*) Candy?

She goes

SCENE 5

Music. Mists, general magic and great beauty of atmosphere

Beauty's bed is transferred magically to her own bedroom and the sounds change to early morning noises like cock-crow. She sits up in bed and looks around. There is a chest by her bed

Beauty It's happened. Here I am at home. (*She rings the bell*) Mrs Buller! Mrs Buller!

Mrs Buller and Arnold appear outside the door

Mrs Buller Did you hear a bell?
Arnold Yes.
Mrs Buller There's nobody in there. It's Beauty's room.
Arnold Then it must be her ghost.

Mrs Buller Don't be ridiculous. Life would be terribly overcrowded if everyone kept turning up after they were supposed to be gone. (*She goes in*)

Beauty Good-morning, Mrs Buller.

Mrs Buller Aaaaah! It is a ghost! Save me Arnold.

Arnold You great big baby.

Beauty I'm not a ghost. I'm alive and as happy as can be.

Arnold It's Miss Beauty. How lovely to see you. (*He kisses her*)

Mrs Buller Has she got all her arms and legs? He's not torn out her entrails or turned her into a zombie?

Beauty Of course not. You can kiss me if you like.

Mrs Buller Oh! It is you. No-one but you would ever say that. Oh my darling girl. (*She goes and kisses Beauty*)

Arnold (*calling*) Mr Smith! It's Beauty, back home, alive and well, and kissing Mrs Buller, which may kill her off properly.

Mrs Buller You should be dead, you know. That was the arrangement, off to the Beast to die.

Beauty It turned out quite differently.

Mrs Buller Well, now you're here you're going to stay. We'll fatten you up, and take you for walks, and let you practise the harpsichord——

Beauty I'm only here for a week, Mrs Buller, I've promised.

Mrs Buller If I say you're going to stay, you're going to stay. (*To the audience*) Isn't she? Isn't she? (*Emphatically*) She's going to stay in this nice tidy house, where people look after her properly and see she cleans her finger-nails, and that is absolutely that. Pick up those ears.

Beauty You haven't changed, have you.

Mrs Buller Certainly not.

Arnold She was frightened just now.

Mrs Buller I was not!

Mr Smith enters

Mr Smith What is it? Oh! Oh, my Beauty!

Beauty Papa, I've come specially to see you.

Mr Smith (*tearful*) Oh my girl.

Mrs Buller (*to Arnold*) Don't gawp. And you've got dandruff.

Arnold And you were frightened.

Mrs Buller Stop saying that!

Mr Smith But didn't that awful creature kill you?

Beauty He's not awful. He's kind and sweet. And I've come home to see you for a whole week just to show you that.

Mr Smith Oh my love.

Beauty Oh Papa.

Ivy (*off*) Hello-o.

Arnold Ah. We've had the ointment. Here come the flies.

Jacintha (*off*) Hello-o.

Ivy (*off*) What's everyone doing up there-ere?

Mrs Buller Come and see-ee.

Ivy
Jacintha } (*together, off*) We wi-ill.

They enter

Ivy Oh, look what the cat's brought in. It's Butter Wouldn't Melt In Your Mouth again.

Jacintha What happened? Did he spew you up? Too pious to keep down, were you?

Mrs Buller She was too good to eat.

Mr Smith Oh, my love.

Beauty Oh, Papa.

Arnold She's only here for a week, so you be nice to her.

Ivy Who are you talking to?

Mr Smith Please remember it's lovely to see her. Oh my love.

Beauty Oh, Papa.

Mrs Buller And she's staying here, please note, for ever.

Arnold Will that be all right, d'you think?

Mrs Buller If I say so.

Jacintha (*peering*) Is she all there? Nothing missing?

Ivy (*peering too*) Didn't the Beast attack you?

Beauty Of course not. He's gentle, and kind and generous, and interested in books and music and things like that.

Ivy Boring as well as beastly.

Mrs Buller Some Beasts can be deceptively nice.

Arnold Mr Buller for example?

Mrs Buller (*big put down*) He had a heart of gold.

Jacintha Well, Father brought us back a lot of gold from this old Beast last time, so what's he sent now? (*She peers at the chest*) chest!

Beauty Open it and see. — IVY Oa, another chest!

Ivy Oooh. A little mirror.

Jacintha And dresses and trinkets and lots of tiny knick-knacks with diamonds on them.

Ivy All for you are they? *they could be but,*

Beauty I don't want them. You have them.

Ivy
Jacintha } (*together*) Good!

The plunge their hands into the chest. There is a great flash and the chest slams shut trapping their hands. A low growl

Mr Smith Look!

Ivy
Jacintha } (*together*) Ow, oh, ooh, help ... *etc.*

Mrs Buller (*alarmed and looking around*) It's him! You see? She's not going back to that.

Arnold You're right, she's not.

Beauty He's just playing games, that's all.

Jacintha Help us, Arnold, it's hurting.

Ivy Lift the lid.

Arnold It won't lift.

Mrs Buller Pull them instead.

Jacintha No. Oh. You're pulling our hands off.

Arnold You never use them, anyway.

Mr Smith Oh dear. They're stuck.

Arnold Bad luck, I'm afraid.

Ivy Well somebody do something. My back's breaking.

Arnold Really?

Mr Smith Perhaps the Beast meant them for you, and no-one else must touch them.

Beauty ~~Yes. Especially not them. He hates them.~~ *Probably. He does hate Ivy & Jacintha.*

Arnold He's got taste then.

Beauty (*calling*) Thank you, Beast, I'll wear the dresses and I'll be home soon.

A low growl. The chest flies open and the sisters are released

Mrs Buller (*alarmed*) Goodness. He's all over the place.

Mr Smith How alarming.

Beauty He only does that sort of thing with the presents he sends. (*She chuckles*) Help me dress, Mrs Buller, and then I'll say hello to the husbands.

Mrs Buller I don't feel entirely at ease.

Arnold You're frightened.

Mrs Buller I'm not!

Mrs Buller and Beauty go off

Jacintha Ivy, a plan occurs to me.

Ivy Poison?

Jacintha Much better. If we make our dummy little sister happy here, and persuade her to stay longer than a week——

Ivy (*appalled*) Longer?

Jacintha Yes longer. Then her Beast, who evidently has a very short temper with people he dislikes, will get very very cross indeed.

Ivy Oh!

Jacintha And he might be tempted to——

Ivy
Jacintha } (*together*)—eat her all up.

Horrid laughs

Ivy Right. Splendid. We'll do it.

Mrs Buller peers in

Mrs Buller Thought of something joyous have you? A new way of cheating at snakes and ladders?

Jacintha We're just so happy our sister's here.

Arnold
Mrs Buller } (*together*) Happy?

Ivy Aren't you?

Mrs Buller I am yes, but——
Sir Thomas (*off*) Yoohoo!
Sir Simon (*off*) What are you doing?
Jacintha Oh, we're having a lovely time, Thomas, come and see.
Ivy Do come, Simon.
Arnold What's the matter with them?
Mr Smith They're happy to have Beauty home.

Sir Simon and Sir Thomas enter

Mrs Buller goes off

Sir Thomas Here's today's joke. What do you get if you cross a steam-roller
with a hippopotamus?
Sir Simon I don't know. What do you get if you cross a steam-roller with a
hippopotamus?
Sir Thomas Ivy. Or Jacintha. Ha, ha, ha!

Sir Simon laughs

Jacintha Darling boy.
Ivy Dearest lamb.
Jacintha You'll never guess what a lovely surprise we've got for you.
Sir Simon Divorce proceedings?
Ivy
Jacintha } (*together*) Our sister Beauty.
Sir Simon Oh. The nice one.

Beauty appears in finery, with Mrs Buller

Mrs Buller And here she is.
Mr Smith Oh my love!
Beauty Oh Papa!
Sir Thomas But you've been digested.
Beauty Of course I haven't. And congratulations on your marriages, (*she
kisses each*) Simon and Thomas.
Sir Simon Oh!
Sir Thomas Oh!
Sir Simon D'you think she'll come and play games with us?
Mrs Buller Perhaps she will.
Ivy She will.
Jacintha Just ask her.
Arnold And then she *will* stay with us for ever.
Mrs Buller Yes!
Ivy
Jacintha } (*together*) Yes! For ever! (*They laugh*)
Mrs Buller What is it with you two?

Song 14: Playing Silly Games

Sir Simon ⎰ We want to play
Sir Thomas ⎱ Silly games all day—

Marbles, conkers,
Musical bumps.

They make us ill
'Cos they never will
Join in the fun,
So we're in the dumps.

We can't get enough
Of Blindman's Buff,
Hopscotch, Who's On,
All that stuff,
So come and have a romp
'Til we're out of puff—
Playing silly games all day—
We're playing silly games all day.

Sir Simon
Sir Thomas   We're full of beans
Beauty   So we'll play Sardines,
Follow My Leader
Postman's Knock.

All of the week
We will Hide and Seek
Grandmother's Footsteps,
What a shock.

If the weather's wrong
Outside, we long
For Ludo, Cluedo,
Chess, Mah Jong,

Hunting for the Slipper,
Or Pinging the Pong—
Playing silly games all day—
We're playing silly games all day.

All   See how we cope
With a skipping rope
Frisbee, hoopla,
Skittles and bowls.

If off we roam
Forty Forty Home
Will keep us amused
On our evening strolls.

POSSIBLE CHANGE
We'll Three-Legged-Race
Till we're blue in the face
To keep us amused
On our evening strolls.

And we'll each have a go
With the old Yo-Yo
Whipping at the Top,
Diabolo
Shuttlecock, Battledore,
Tig, oho—

Playing silly games all day;
We're playing silly games all day.

Coda
We know how to fiddle
At Kiss in the Middle,
And have a little dabble
At Halma and Scrabble,
There's Jacks for the nimble,
And Hide the Thimble,
And King of the Castle,
And Passing the Parcel,
And Coppers and Robbing,
And Apples for Bobbing,
We're playing silly games,
Playing silly games,
Playing silly games,
All day!
Playing silly games all day.

Beauty (*speaking*) Oh, that was terrific! (*She chases the two men*)
Sir Simon Oh the joy!
Sir Thomas The ecstasy!
Sir Simon Games!
Beauty I haven't played games for ages! Come on, you two.

She chases Ivy and Jacintha who squawk

Jacintha Oh! Oh dear!
Ivy I hope this works.

The young are off

Arnold It's just lovely to have her back.
Mr Smith Delicious. And I thought I'd never smile again.
Mrs Buller Then that's settled. She must stay with us.
Mr Smith She can't stay. She has to go back at the end of the week, keeping her word.
Mrs Buller She's done that already once. You can't go on making bargains with people who want to kill you. It's sloppy thinking.
Mr Smith But he's magic. You saw how he shut that chest up even though he wasn't here. He'll kill her from afar. He's all powerful and all awful.
Arnold I tell you what, Mrs Buller can go to the castle and talk to him and explain we want to keep Beauty here.
Mrs Buller Talk to him? To the Beast?
Arnold Unless you're frightened of course.
Mrs Buller I'm not frightened of anything. All right. I'll go.
Arnold Brave lady!
Mrs Buller In a day or two. About ten, probably. I'll go and tell him he's had his chance to murder Beauty, and now it's too late. I know how to deal with Beasts and don't you say another word.

Mr Smith Well, do be careful, Mrs Buller, because it'll be very difficult to find someone to replace you.
Mrs Buller Impossible.

Beauty bursts in

Beauty Come on, Arnold, It's hide and seek. (*She grabs him*)
Arnold It's wonderful!
Beauty And you two as well. Oh this is fun. Whee!
Arnold Great joy!

Beauty goes with Arnold

Mrs Buller (*pulling Mr Smith*) All right then! Let's enjoy the chaos for a mad while. Whee!

They go too

SCENE 6

Frontcloth

Snowdrop enters

Snowdrop Candy! Candy! It's going wrong, and we're going to lose everything.

Candy is in the audience

Candy I'm afraid you're in that by yourself now, dear, because I'm rather busy saving the masses from the Yuk Potion. Can I just have a show of hands for who's had the ice-cream, please?
Snowdrop Candy!
Candy Ice-cream eaters? Oh, I can see. Some of you have got scales all over. Fingers turning to claws. Ears going all furry. Toes, anyone got fewer toes than when they came in? No need to take your shoes off, dear, you can tell by wiggling them. And the beer drinkers? Yes, you've got your come uppance, haven't you. That nose may never be the same again. Those glazed eyes aren't going to focus in a hurry. Now the only way to stop the mass Beast Transformation is——
Snowdrop Candy—how can you do this to me?
Candy Quiet. The only way to stop the mass Beast Transformation is the reciting of this little spell. Abracadabra, alikazoo, Yuk we've had enough of you.
Snowdrop You're totally missing the point.
Candy Just be helpful for a change, will you Snowdrop, so we can save all these nice people from being beasts.
Snowdrop This is not the way to do it.
Candy And don't argue in public. (*To the audience*) Are you ready? After three. One, two, three.

Business

A bit louder.

Again business

Yes, right, exactly. That should do it permanently this time. There are still some flaring nostrils around, and some unsightly feathers, but they'll go eventually. I think that's settled Dolores's hash. (*She laughs*)

Dolores enters pushing a large box

Dolores Oh, no, no, no. Oh dear me no. I'm just perfecting Yuk Potion Mark Three, which is much stronger. You won't be able to find anything to put that right at all.

Candy I'm the best good fairy in the business and I have made these people safe from any Yuk Potion you can think of.

Dolores Well, then let's see if that's true, shall we?

Snowdrop Candy, this could be serious.

Dolores It is, Lotus Blossom, it is. Can I have two daring little people from the audience?

Candy You have no faith, Snowdrop. My magic will protect these little ones. Come along, dears, have no fear. Your Aunty Candy will look after you.

Two children come up from the audience

Dolores And so will your Aunty Dolores. What's your name then, sunshine? And yours, honeybunch? Fond of your friends and things are you? Well, just wave goodbye to them.

Candy Don't worry. You're quite safe.

Dolores Safe as your granny bending down in front of an express train. Now if you'll just step inside here. (*She shows them into the box*) That's right. And then I'll just spray in this experimental dose of Yuk Potion Mark Three.

Snowdrop This is a disaster, I know.

Candy Nothing can possibly happen, dear girl.

An immense flash. A lot of whirring, some mysterious music then another flash

Snowdrop You see? It's going to be horrid.

Dolores That's right.

Snowdrop We should have concentrated on getting Beauty back from the Beast.

Candy Don't be repetitive.

Dolores One more drop——

Another flash

And if you'd just step out and show us your lovely little innocent faces. There.

The two children reappear as beasts

Candy Oh my sainted spell-book!

Dolores Isn't it a shame, eh? Really horrible. And they might have grown up quite pretty if they hadn't been coaxed up here by you. Now, once I mass produce this stuff, I'll have you all beasts in what we call a trice. Come along with me, my dears, and I'll put you away for ever in a lonely castle while I make a few more gallons of nastiness. Cheer up, Wallflower.

She leads the children away

Snowdrop I knew you'd get the whole thing utterly wrong.
Candy Then you should have said something. It's all very serious and we'll have to take action. Think.
Snowdrop Me?
Candy Yes you, Buttercup. Don't always leave it to other people.
Snowdrop That's not fair! I've been trying to tell you for the last five minutes—the week has passed, Beauty hasn't gone back, only Mrs Buller, on that silly bicycle! We're too late!
Candy (*leaving*) Then it's time to hide again.
Snowdrop (*leaving*) No!

They exit

Scene 7

The Beast's courtyard. All as before and the mirror in evidence

Mrs Buller bicycles in, and dismounts

Mrs Buller Well, it doesn't look too bad at all. Oh, a mirror. That could do with a bit of a dust. It's a bit cloudy. (*She breathes on it and rubs it*)

We see Beauty and her sisters and hear them laughing

Ivy Come on, another game of hunt the thimble.
Beauty Oh, I don't know when I've been so happy.

The picture fades

Mrs Buller Good heavens! (*She rubs the mirror again*) Come on, I want to see that. Come on! Show me, show me!

She rubs it again. No use

The Beast enters all sad and wan

Beast Don't. It only shows things that hurt.
Mrs Buller Needs a good kick, I expect. Go on, you silly machine. (*She gives it one then realizes she is with the Beast*) Aaah! You're the Beast!
Beast And you're Mrs Buller. That makes two of us. Hahaha. Clever little joke.
Mrs Buller Really.
Beast I'm not in the mood to explain.
Mrs Buller If I may say so, you look rather run down for a beast.
Beast She's stayed at home, hasn't she, so I'm broken-hearted.

Mrs Buller Now that's just an attitude of mind. What you need is a nice cup of tea, a biscuit, then a long walk in the country.

Beast No.

Mrs Buller Is the kitchen this way?

Beast I said no!

Mrs Buller Suit yourself. I'm here to explain things to you.

Beast She's left me, hasn't she. I hoped she loved me, Mrs Buller, and I never should have!

Mrs Buller Oh come now, I won't have people insinuating nasty things about——

Beast She left me like any flighty young thing!

Mrs Buller If you say that I'll make you kiss me.

The Beast turns away in disgust

You should be so lucky.

Beast My luck was to have one dear friend. Now she's gone and there's nothing left for me. (*Tears*)

Mrs Buller Oh, don't do that. There's me. And if you really wanted, you could whisk her back by magic.

Beast But I love her. You don't play tricks like that on people you love.

Mrs Buller You don't?

Beast Her sisters play tricks on her. All that lovey-dovey nonsense for instance—look. (*He causes the mirror to flash on again*)

We see Ivy and Jacintha sniggering

Ivy He'll come and eat her soon, now she's let him down.

Jacintha He's very slow about it. Not much of a beast, if you ask me.

Ivy Don't worry. He'll take his revenge, bound to.

The mirror goes off

Mrs Buller (*going for her bike*) Well I never. I'll put a stop to that. I'll see Beauty knows what's what and send her back to you.

Beast If she wanted to come back, she'd've looked in the little mirror I gave her, but she hasn't and that's that.

Mrs Buller That is not that! Just pull your socks up and I'll bicycle home and——

Beast I can't pull my socks up, I'm dying! It's what you do when you love people and they don't love you back. I'm dying, I'm dying, I'm dying! (*And he cries tears and sighs*)

Mrs Buller For heaven's sake, you wishy-washy Beast! Oh, the chaos, the mess. (*She turns to the mirror*) Come on, work, work.

She kicks it and it flickers into life

We see Beauty playing a game

Look in your little mirror. Go on look! Come on shout.

The audience join in

Snowdrop appears and encourages everyone but to no avail

Dolores appears with a huge fly spray

Dolores It's no use. She can't hear you.

Beauty looks in the mirror and adjusts her hair, then hears someone and runs off happily, chased by Sir Simon and Sir Thomas

Mrs Buller (*during this*) Beauty, he's dying. He's dying. Dy-ing!
Dolores You see?
Mrs Buller Who are you?
Dolores I am a supernatural being.
Mrs Buller Well you're making a mess of things, as usual.
Dolores I hope so. I've brewed a lot of Yuk Potion Mark Three so that in a moment the whole lot of you will be like the other two.

Candy appears

Candy (*startled*) What?

Dolores is brandishing her syringe

Snowdrop I challenge you, Dolores.
Dolores Foxglove?
Snowdrop (*to Dolores*) I know how to defeat you, and my name is Snowdrop. Give us a song-sheet.
Candy (*taking charge rather*) Yes, right, exactly. Give us a song-sheet.

This appears, masking the Beast

Dolores Oh, that old trick. There won't be anyone left to sing when I've finished. I'll just get my spray of the Yuk Potion Mark Three and that'll settle everything.

She goes off

Mrs Buller Are we at that woman's mercy?
Candy Certainly not.
Mrs Buller Good. She needs to see someone. Who are you?
Snowdrop If we all sing this and you make beast noises as loudly as you can, Beauty will hear and look in her little mirror. Because, sometimes, beast noises get through to her. This is how it goes.

Song 15: Beast Noises (*as printed on the song-sheet*)

Snowdrop	Beasts make a terrible growl—Grrrr, Grrrr.
Candy	Unless they're cross and then they howl—owww owwww.
Mrs Buller	But when they're feeling sad they cry
	With a noise that brings tears to every eye,
	It's a bit of a wail and a bit of a sigh—
	Aaaah, aaaaah.

Dolores enters with her syringe and a bucket of Yuk Potion Mark Three

Dolores Not a chance she'll hear that. Here we go. (*She fills the spray and squirts the audience. She does this again and again with increased vigour throughout, laughing madly*)

Snowdrop Get singing all of you.
Mrs Buller Come on take those sweets out of your mouths ... *etc.*
Candy Open your mouths, dears. Let the notes come through ... *etc.*

*During this, the mirror flickers as Beauty keeps appearing and stops as if
hearing something, dismissing it and passing on her way*

Snowdrop Louder. (*Then*) We nearly did it. (*Then*) One more time. (*Then*)
There. She's heard.
Beauty Oh. The Beast! I'd forgotten him! Where's the mirror he gave me?

She runs out of sight

Dolores Oh bum! Really wobbly buttocks and old toe-nails!
Snowdrop Who's a mere apprentice, then? Who can't beat an experienced
old witch?

She points at Dolores and the spray explodes

No more Yuk Potion, and everyone's safe.
Dolores Warts and bogeys.
Candy Well done, Snowdrop.
Mrs Buller Oh very well done. Are there many openings in the good fairy
business?
Candy Only for the young and beautiful. And I always said the young and
beautiful Snowdrop was promising, didn't I?
Snowdrop When?
Candy Didn't I? Yes, right, exactly. Now go and get those children, dear, or
their parents will be wanting their money back.

Snowdrop goes off

Dolores Can't I keep them?
Mrs Buller What sort of a mother would you make?
Dolores Like to be a witch fairy, would you?
Mrs Buller Go away!

Snowdrop comes back with the children

Candy Come along, my little poppets. We'll take you back where you
belong. Aren't they handsome and pretty? Oh, the treasures.
Mrs Buller I could eat them. Oh—I mean—haha.

Mrs Buller and the good fairies return the children

Dolores is left alone

Dolores I hope you don't think you're going to get the soppy ending.
They've taken so long over all that, my Beast is very nearly dead. (*She
smiles*) Lovely. Of course, that means I'll have to get another husband,
but there's one down there I've got my eye on. See you later, gorgeous,
and don't you refuse me, because I still know a nasty trick or two.

She chuckles and goes

Beauty now returns again behind the magic mirror and has her own smaller mirror in her hand

Beauty Now, let me look.

The Beast can be heard sighing

Oh Beast, you're ill. I'd forgotten you, and you're ill. Let me be with you. I want to be with you more than I want anything else. You're the person I love most in the whole world.

Music. She steps through the mirror into the courtyard. The song sheet goes up and the Beast is revealed dying. He holds a rose

Beast Beauty? You came back?
Beauty Of course I did.
Beast You forgot your promise, and I was so upset. Now I've seen you again, I'm happy, and I can die happy. Here, take this rose.
Beauty Beast, please live and be my love. I thought you were only my friend, but now I know I can't ever live without you. From this moment, I swear to be none but yours.

She kisses him. After she has done this, the castle sparkles with light, there are fireworks and great music. She looks up from her kiss

What is it? What's happening?

The Beast arises now as King Tom

Tom I'm happening. You've freed me from a wicked curse by loving me. And I have to confess, I love you, too. I do do that sort of thing after all.
Beauty You're wearing funny clothes.
Tom And my face has changed.
Beauty Has it? It still looks kind and gentle to me.
Tom It's a king's face. I'm a king. King Tom of Belldrovia.
Beauty If you're as kind and thoughtful and altogether beautiful when you are King Tom as you were before, it doesn't make any difference, does it. You're still the beast I loved. (*She kisses him*)

Mrs Buller enters

Mrs Buller Though as a matter of fact, I was rather more taken with him as he was. He reminded me of certain things.

The whole cast now appear

Dolores The whole thing is appallingly sentimental.
Candy (*wiping her eyes*) There's nothing wrong with sentiment. And I've brought along all your family to weep and cry with joy because it's all turned out so happily.

Tears

Mr Smith Oh my love.
Beauty (*still gazing at Tom in love*) Oh Papa.

Tom Pardon?

Beauty I mean oh Tom! I really do.

Candy I'm afraid there is one rather nasty job left to do. Ivy and Jacintha, you've been absolutely rotten throughout this whole affair.

Ivy
Jacintha } (*together*) We haven't.

Candy They have, haven't they. Haven't they?

Snowdrop They have.

Candy Yes right exactly. So you are to become statues outside your sister's gates until you admit your faults.

Sir Thomas Oh good!

Ivy (*as she freezes*) But we were normal.

Jacintha (*as she freezes*) Normal and selfish.

Snowdrop They'll never learn, I'm afraid.

Sir Simon I hope not.

Candy Meanwhile, I'll proclaim you King Tom of Belldrovia.

Tom And I shall try to be the kindest, sweetest ruler it ever had.

Dolores Oh yuk! Everybody looking pretty and thoroughly fulfilled. What a bore!

Beauty And I shall see that he really keeps his promise. Oh Tom, I think you're absolutely a knock-out.

Song 16: Just the Way You Are

(*Singing*)   The way that you look is marvellous
                     But it's skin deep and no more.
                     If you are a king,
                     Well, that's a thing
                     I'll try not to find a bore.
                     But what you must remember
                     Is a lovelier thing by far;
                     That under the spell,
                     The thing that I fell for
                     Was simply the way you are.

                     Chorus
                     I like you just the way you are,
                     'Cos what you do the way you are
                     Is make me glad to be
                     The way we had to be,
                     Never sad to be the way we are.

Tom   I trust us just the way we are.
                     No fuss, it's just the way we are.
                     You make me want to say
                     I always want to stay
                     Ever and a day the way we are.

Sir Thomas   Though we like being free
Sir Simon }   We're lonely as can be.
                     Fed up,

	We miss our loving cup.
	French cricket just doesn't make up for it.
Candy	Oh well,
Snowdrop	We'll take off the spell.
	Just promise you won't scream and yell.
Jacintha	Yes please,
Ivy	We promise not to tease.
	You'll love to squeeze us just the way we are.

Chorus

Ivy, Jacintha We like us just the way we are,
Sir Thomas No fuss it's just the way we are.
Sir Simon It makes us glad to be
The way it had to be;
Never sad to be the way we are.

Mr Smith Great joy,
Nothing can cloy.
Each daughter has found a nice boy.

Arnold Hold on.
Now that they are gone
Won't you be sad on your own?

Mrs Buller Oh no.
I'll never go.
No bossing, I shall cosset him so.

Mr Smith All three,
Mrs Buller Quite a family,
Arnold We're happy just to be the way we are.

Chorus
We like us just the way we are,
No fuss it's just the way we are.
It makes us glad to be
The way it had to be;
Never sad to be the way we are.

Dolores Oh yuk
Rubbishy muck.
I hope some day that they will all come unstuck.
I'm not
Going to change a jot.
My one ambition is to ruin this lot.

Beauty All through the evil of you
Tom We have discovered a love that is true.
Fume as you may
We would like to say
We're happy that you stay the way you are.

Chorus
All We like us just the way we are,
No fuss it's just the way we are.

It makes us glad to be
The way it had to be,
Never sad to be the way we are.

(*To the*   And we like you just the way you are,
audience)   'Cos what you do the way you are
Is make us glad to be
The way it had to be,
Never sad to be the way we are.
We're happy just to be the way we are!

CURTAIN

FURNITURE AND PROPERTY LIST

ACT I

SCENE 1

On stage: Throne
Papers, pen for **Tom**
Crown

Personal: **Dolores:** gin bottle (optional)
Tom: glasses

SCENE 2

On stage: Chair
Table. *On it:* eyeshades, chocolates
Harpsichord
Stool
Duster for **Arnold**
Window curtains (*closed*)

Off stage: 2 chaise-longues **(Arnold)**
Documents **(Snowdrop)**

Personal: **Mrs Buller:** belt with keys, watch on breast
Sir Thomas: coin

SCENE 3

On stage: Hammock attached to 2 tree trunks
Glass connected to vat of gin
Sweets for **Dolores**

SCENE 4

On stage: Haystacks
Hayforks

Off stage: Penny-farthing bicycle **(Arnold)**

SCENE 5

On stage: Trees

Off stage: Bicycle **(Mr Smith)**

SCENE 6

On stage: Door with grille
Rose bushes and trees

Off stage: Bicycle **(Mr Smith)**
Table set with food, chair **(Stage Management)**
Wine **(Stage Management)**
Chest **(Stage Management)**

Personal: **Beast:** eyes that can glow when required

SCENE 7

Off stage: Hammock **(Dolores)**

SCENE 8

On stage: Chest full of jewels, bags of gold, clothes
Stool

Off stage: Bicycle **(Arnold)**

Personal: **Arnold:** handkerchief
Jacintha: onions

SCENE 9

No props required

SCENE 10

On stage: Door with grille
Rose bushes and trees
Table with place laid
Chair
Harpsichord
Large mirror
Shelf with books
Presents

Off stage: Bicycle **(Beauty)**
Food **(Stage Management)**

ACT II

PROLOGUE

On stage: Hammock
Gin for **Dolores**

SCENE 1

On stage: As Act I, Scene 2, plus:
              Extra dressing
              Wedding food

SCENE 2

No props required

SCENE 3

On stage: As Act I, Scene 10

Off stage: Hand mirror **(Stage Management)**
              Comb **(Stage Management)**
              Garland of roses **(Stage Management)**

SCENE 4

On stage: Bed and bedding (*behind frontcloth*)

Personal: **Dolores:** gin bottle

SCENE 5

On stage: Bed and bedding
              Chest. *On it:* small bell. *In it:* hand mirror, dresses, trinkets, jewellery, *etc.*

SCENE 6

Off stage: Large box (*with 2 beast masks inside*), syringe/spray of Yuk Potion Mark
              Three

SCENE 7

On stage: As Act I, Scene 10

Off stage: Huge syringe/spray **(Dolores)**
              Song-sheet **(Stage Management)**
              Bucket, syringe **(Dolores)**
              Hand mirror **(Beauty)**

Personal: **Beast:** rose

LIGHTING PLOT

Practical fittings required: *nil*

ACT I

To open: Darkness

Cue 1	**After flash and crack of thunder** *Snap up spot on* **Dolores**	(Page 1)
Cue 2	**Dolores:** "... like me could want." Trumpets *Bring up lights on coronation*	(Page 1)
Cue 3	**Dolores** exits *Cut spot*	(Page 1)
Cue 4	**Dolores:** "There!" *Bring up outline of grim and gloomy castle upstage*	(Page 2)
Cue 5	**Dolores** laughs and is gone *Cross-fade to lighting downstage on* **Candy** *and* **Snowdrop**	(Page 2)
Cue 6	**Candy:** "Let's have a look, shall we?" *Bring up lighting on* **Smiths**' *drawing-room*	(Page 3)
Cue 7	**Arnold** opens curtains *Increase lighting*	(Page 4)
Cue 8	**Mrs Buller** closes curtains *Decrease lighting*	(Page 6)
Cue 9	As Scene 3 opens *Change to lighting on hammock and frontcloth area*	(Page 14)
Cue 10	As Scene 4 opens *General exterior lighting*	(Page 15)
Cue 11	As Scene 5 opens *Gloomy lighting, with flashes of lightning*	(Page 18)
Cue 12	As **Mr Smith** arrives in courtyard of **Beast**'s Castle *Change to bright sunny lighting*	(Page 18)
Cue 13	As **Beast** smashes down door *Light above and behind him*	(Page 19)
Cue 14	As **Beast** moves into courtyard *Cut light above and behind him*	(Page 19)
Cue 15	As Scene 7 opens *Frontcloth lighting*	(Page 21)
Cue 16	As Scene 8 opens *General lighting*	(Page 22)

Cue 17	As Scene 9 opens	(Page 25)
	Frontcloth lighting	
Cue 18	As Scene 10 opens	(Page 26)
	Bright, lovely lighting on courtyard	
Cue 19	**Beauty:** ". . . know what he's doing."	(Page 26)
	Mirror glows, revealing **Mr Smith** *and* **Mrs Buller** *behind it*	
Cue 20	**Mr Smith:** "I wish we weren't."	(Page 26)
	Fade lighting on mirror	

ACT II

Cue 21	When ready	(Page 30)
	Lights up on **Dolores**	
Cue 22	As Scene 1 opens	(Page 30)
	Change to general interior lighting	
Cue 23	As Scene 2 opens	(Page 33)
	Frontcloth lighting	
Cue 24	As Scene 3 opens	(Page 34)
	Lighting on courtyard	
Cue 25	As Scene 4 opens	(Page 37)
	Frontcloth lighting	
Cue 26	Frontcloth goes up	(Page 38)
	Dim lighting on bed	
Cue 27	As Scene 5 opens	(Page 39)
	Magical lighting on bed, then change to general morning light	
Cue 28	As Scene 6 opens	(Page 46)
	Frontcloth lighting	
Cue 29	As Scene 7 opens	(Page 48)
	Lighting on courtyard	
Cue 30	**Mrs Buller** breathes on mirror and rubs it	(Page 48)
	Mirror glows, revealing **Beauty** *and her sisters behind it*	
Cue 31	**Beauty:** ". . . I've been so happy."	(Page 48)
	Fade lighting on mirror	
Cue 32	**Beast:** ". . . for instance—look."	(Page 49)
	Mirror glows, revealing **Ivy** *and* **Jacintha** *behind it*	
Cue 33	**Ivy:** ". . . his revenge, bound to."	(Page 49)
	Fade lighting on mirror	
Cue 34	**Mrs Buller** kicks mirror	(Page 49)
	Mirror glows, revealing **Beauty** *behind it*	
Cue 35	**Beauty** runs off happily	(Page 50)
	Fade lighting on mirror	
Cue 36	As **Mrs Buller** and **Candy** encourage the audience to sing	(Page 51)
	Mirror flickers as **Beauty** *keeps appearing and passing on her way, then mirror glows up full*	

Cue 37	**Beauty** runs out of sight *Fade lighting on mirror*	(Page 51)
Cue 38	**Dolores** chuckles and goes *Mirror glows, revealing* **Beauty**	(Page 51)
Cue 39	**Beauty** steps through mirror *Fade lighting on mirror*	(Page 52)
Cue 40	**Beauty** kisses **Beast** *Castle sparkles with light*	(Page 52)

EFFECTS PLOT

ACT I

Cue 1   As Scene 1 opens   (Page 1)
Flash, crack of thunder

Cue 2   **Dolores**: "... like me could want."   (Page 1)
Trumpets

Cue 3   **Another Courtier**: "Yes, Your Majesty."   (Page 1)
Flash

Cue 4   **Dolores**: "You're not normal!"   (Page 2)
Great crash, followed by strange sounds

Cue 5   **Dolores**: "There!"   (Page 2)
Mist

Cue 6   **All** (*singing*): "Beautiful and rich."   (Page 9)
Bell rings loudly

Cue 7   **Dolores**: "... his temper is awful. Listen!"   (Page 14)
Howl, off

Cue 8   As Scene 5 opens   (Page 18)
Storm noises

Cue 9   **Snowdrop**: "... all depressed and sad."   (Page 18)
More storm noises

Cue 10   **Snowdrop**: "He's near the castle."   (Page 18)
More storm noises

Cue 11   As Scene 6 opens   (Page 18)
Storm noises, Bicycle Song, low growl, then fade

Cue 12   **Mr Smith** takes a rose   (Page 19)
Terrific roar

Cue 13   **Beauty**: "... that Papa picked for me."   (Page 26)
Harpsichord plays "A Rose is a Rose"

Cue 14   **Beauty**: "... being away from him."   (Page 26)
Sounds of **Beast** *arriving*

ACT II

Cue 15   As Prologue opens   (Page 30)
Flash

Cue 16   **Dolores**: "... self-interested weddings."   (Page 30)
Sound of wedding bells

MADE AND PRINTED IN GREAT BRITAIN BY
LATIMER TREND & COMPANY LTD PLYMOUTH
MADE IN ENGLAND

Preset: Pf. Tina 081